CLOSE ENOUGH TO PERFECT

CLOSE ENOUGH TO PERFECT

a true story of love, grief, resilience & spirit

Christine Noyes

Haley's
Athol, Massachusetts

© 2021 by Christine Noyes.

All rights reserved. With the exception of short excerpts in a review or critical article, no part of this book may be re-produced by any means, including information storage and retrieval or photocopying equipment, without written permission of the publisher, Haley's.

Haley's
488 South Main Street
Athol, MA 01331
haley.antique@verizon.net • 978.249.9400

Copy edited by Ellen Woodbury. Proof read by Richard Bruno.
Photos from the collection of Christine Noyes unless otherwise credited.

"Unchained Melody" written by Hy Zaret and Alex North. © 1955 (renewed) HZUM Publishing (SESAC) and North Melody Publishing (SESAC) c/o Unchained Melody Publishing LLC All Rights Reserved. Used By Permission.

Library of Congress Cataloging-in-Publication Data
Names: Noyes, Christine, 1961- author.
Title: Close enough to perfect : a true story of love, grief, resilience & spirit / Christine Noyes.
Description: Athol, Massachusetts : Haley's, [2021] | Summary: "Christine
  Noyes shares the story of her loving marriage with Al Noyes and their
  enjoyment of fun-filled travel and adventure until his sudden 2018 death
  aboard a commercial airliner in flight. The author tells of her grief
  and of facing productive life without her loving husband"-- Provided by
  publisher.
Identifiers: LCCN 2020034392 (print) | LCCN 2020034393 (ebook) | ISBN
  9781948380348 (trade paperback) | ISBN 9781948380355 (hardcover) | ISBN
  9781948380362 (pdf)
Subjects: LCSH: Noyes, Christine, 1961- | Noyes, Christine,
  1961---Marriage. | Noyes, Al (Albert E.), 1957-2018. | Widows--United
  States--Biography. | Authors, American--21st century--Biography. | Women
  authors, American--Biography. | Husbands--Death--Psychological aspects.
  | Grief.
Classification: LCC CT275.N7846 A3 2021 (print) | LCC CT275.N7846 (ebook)
  | DDC 306.88/3092 [B]--dc23
LC record available at https://lccn.loc.gov/2020034392
LC ebook record available at https://lccn.loc.gov/2020034393

For Al,
my everything

Lonely rivers flow
to the sea, to the sea—
to the open arms of the sea.
Lonely rivers sigh
"Wait for me, wait for me.
I'll be coming home. Wait for me."

—"Unchained Melody"
Alex North / Hyman Zaret

Contents

Walking Each Other Home xiii
    a foreword by Paula Francis

A Satisfying Cocktail 1
    an introduction by Christine Noyes

Close Enough to Perfect 3

Until Such Time Your Hand I Hold 171
    an afterword by Christine Noyes

About the Author 179

Acknowledgments 181

Colophon 185

Illustrations

Easter in 1965 13
Chris's First Holy Communion 14
Chris's parents at their wedding 15
Chris's parents, Vern and Joyce 16
celebrating Easter Sunday in the mid sixties 21
Thanksgiving, 1974 23
viewing the Apollo 11 moon landing on TV 32
Camp Calamity 34
more Camp Calamity 37
Chris and Al at their 1989 wedding 44
Al's Wyoming antelope 46
Al's birthday "surprise" 57
Al, ever the good sport 57
"Speed—the Ride" 59
NASCAR photo booth photo 61
Chris and Al at her dad's in 1987 63

Al's Jiffy Pop dance..69
the camp cohort...70
Al rocking his floral wreath............................71
The Case of the Missing Cooler........................73
at The Pike restaurant in Gettysburg...............78
Phil Johnson and Al with their catch..............86
Al in his element on the lake..........................88
Al, Chris, Mary, and Vern in the Smoky Mountains 99
Mary and Al..106
Al and Vern—Big Brother and Little Brother......113
Paula, Vern, and Chris...................................114
Vern, Mary, Chris, and Al.............................115
Mary and Al hug...115
friends with thumbs up and number ones........121
Chris and Al's bikes at Lake Gloriette.............127
Chris's grandfather Vern Johnson Sr..............135
Al's legacy..143
Chris and Madelyn..146
Chris loading her shotgun.............................163
Chris fulfilling Al's wish................................164
the cannon launching Al's ashes across the pond...167
Paula releasing Al's ashes..............................169
Chris's first tattoo...173
Al and Chris...177

Walking Each Other Home

a foreword by Paula Francis

It was four o'clock in the morning when my phone rang. "Well, this isn't good," I thought to myself then said out loud to my sister when I answered it.

"It's not," Chris whispered through tears.

I planned to stay for several more weeks in Hawaii as part of my volunteer work. But when someone you love calls, you answer. And so began a new journey, one parallel to my walk around the country interviewing people about happiness. In that life-altering, unhappy moment I recalled the words of Ram Dass, recently quoted to me, "We're all just walking each other home." But first I had to fly . . . fourteen hours from the tropical beaches of metaphoric heaven to the halls of grief in a North Carolinian hotel.

Chris and Al are people you want to surround yourself with. You can always count on a genuine hug, good drink, and the untarnished truth. You can also expect they will give you the shirts off their backs, which is exactly what they did when my soul was laid bruised and naked. After my marriage abruptly fell apart and our father, for whom I had been caring, subsequently passed, my last vestiges of any security vanished. Generously, Chris and Al offered to take me in, but before I could consider my next move, one of us took flight to the shores of life's literal heaven.

It humbles me to bear witness to such heartache and growth. They co-exist in the house Chris and I share like our differing food preferences and our divergent political views—the one balancing the other only to find, in the end, they are one and the same. And of course, you cannot witness something so profound and not yourself change.

Together, Chris and I manage our separate journeys with the aid of similar maps.

Chris's journey brought her to a world with a highly sought-after, yet rarely found soulmate. Then, like a GPS malfunction, it directed her to a cliff.

When faced with the knowledge that something has gone terribly awry, your choices can seem clouded or clear. I don't know where the map may take my sister. Home, I suspect.

Yes, we are walking each other home.

Chris is my rock, my confidant and inspiration. And I love her . . . and Al . . . dearly.

She is not perfect, but who is? Certainly, she is close enough.

A Satisfying Cocktail

an introduction by Christine Noyes

As a preemptive strike—I realize that Al is holding a bottle of scotch in this book's cover photo. After reading the book, any bourbon purist will feel the need to point that out.

When I began to write my memoir, I did not intend to see it published. I wrote to deal with my grief and keep my husband close. As time passed, I received encouragement from unexpected sources including one dead for nine years, and so I changed my mind.

I learned a lot about myself as I wrote the memoir—mostly that my memory fails me as I edge toward the age of sixty. I search a thesaurus to trigger the word on the tip of my tongue. But in some experiences, I find insight that had eluded me these many years. Some insights came from within. Some came from my sister as we talked about our childhood.

I am blessed. I have loved, and I have been loved. And even though the anguish is almost unbearable at times, memories urge their way through the murkiness to make me laugh or smile.

I recall a line from the wonderful movie, *Steel Magnolias*. One of the characters says, "Laughter through tears is my favorite emotion." I concur that, when those two emotional results mix, they create a satisfying cocktail.

Drink up!

Close Enough to Perfect

It rained the day he died. Not the battering drops of a magnificently fierce midsummer thunderstorm but the gentle mist of an unseasonably tepid January predawn in New England. It was two in the morning on Saturday as Al and I gathered the final few bathroom items to cram into our oversized, airline-approved carry-on bags. One cup of coffee would have to suffice, as we had a ninety-minute drive to the airport. At our age, bathroom stops became more pressing and plentiful on their own, so additional stimulants might prove problematic.

Huh! The things we worry about when we don't know that our lives will soon change forever.

We had performed the same mundane packing routine only six short days before. It was trade show season, and we had no sooner returned from Indianapolis before having to make a quick turnaround from our home on the East Coast and jet off to Las Vegas, an admittedly more motivating destination. Because of the large overlap of manufacturers attending trade shows, sponsors customarily schedule them on back-to-back weekends. The practice makes it easier for exhibitors, sales representatives, and moving companies but much harder on small-business owners who have to pack everything up, go home, unpack, catch up on a week's work, repack, and hop on a plane to the next destination. Exactly what we were forced to do.

We had just returned from the Archery Trade Association Show and, because archery comprised a large part of our small sporting goods business, our existence depended on not missing the chance to see the year's new products, talk directly to designers and manufacturers, and take advantage of exclusive show pricing that allowed us to compete directly with much larger big-box chain stores. Some days, we found ourselves sitting at the lunch table with well-paid buyers from the country's largest sporting goods stores. Other days we ate lunch with married couples who, like us, paid well to be there—all of us retailers just trying to make a living at something we felt passionate about.

The previous week, shortly after we arrived in Indy, something hit me like a tsunami swallowing a resort beach. My body began to shut down. I felt weak, tired, congested, and just plain apathetic. I managed to trudge through the first few days of the convention as we visited the most essential booths, Al doing the wheeling and dealing, me dragging along behind as the washed-up anchor, a remnant of the sandy shore.

I spent the next two trade show days in bed, thus forcing Al to finish our business alone while taking care of me as he had done so well for thirty years.

On the last day of the show, Al wrapped up remaining transactions and returned to my bedside. Later that evening, sometime around six o'clock, he asked if I would mind if he went down to the hotel bar to get something to eat, have a few drinks, and mingle with other archery enthusiasts. Of course, I didn't mind. I would have been right there with him if I hadn't felt like a soggy dishrag.

We had been married for twenty-eight years, and other than a few occasions, we did everything together. We worked together, although Al did have a necessary day job to support our entrepreneurial efforts. We played together: shot sporting clays, rode motorcycles, and went to New England Patriots football games. And we drank together, our new love of bourbon surprising both of us.

Even after twenty-eight years of marriage, finishing each other's sentences, reading each other's thoughts, and sharing each other's proclivities, Al could still astonish me.

I presumed he would go down to the hotel bar and have a few beers or maybe a bourbon or two. After all, it had been a busy week, and he had accomplished a great deal, mostly on his own. I appreciated his need to blow off a little steam, and since he didn't have to drive anywhere, what harm was there? What harm, indeed. Had I not been so far under the weather, I would have seen the warning signs.

After a few hours I began to get annoyed that he had not come back to the room to check on me, and as the clock continued to tick, my annoyance advanced as well.

The hands circled the clock seven times before I heard thumping at the door, the sound of Al trying unsuccessfully to operate his key card. I waited and tried to calm my mixed emotions, both worried and infuriated. The ruckus continued until I gathered the strength to get out of bed and open the door. With his hand on the handle, his substantial body leaning against the door, and no self-control of his own, Al clumsily rode the door into the room. We stood eye to eye for a slight moment before I lost my battle of emotional control and Al lost his battle of balance. I barely got out the words "What the hell?" before he hit the floor.

I am not a slight woman and even if I had felt my best, I knew the high improbability that I could hoist his body, well over three hundred pounds, onto the bed. I moved his feet in order to close the door, placed a pillow under his head, threw a blanket over him, and went back to bed.

I'm sure he was embarrassed and maybe even angry at himself for losing control, as I have felt myself on occasion. Al and I didn't only share the same interests, we also shared many characteristics, one of which I refer to as the tea kettle trait. It may take us a while, but once that kettle sings its crescendo, it pours out of us with uncontrolled fervor, which usually requires a two-day hangover recovery.

Three days later, Al fell victim to my cold.

The sun still slept as we loaded the car, remarkably on schedule, to leave for Las Vegas. Al struggled with his breathing, labored at every movement. Seemingly, he could not inhale enough air to satisfy his need, his cadenced effort going unrewarded.

He had seen the doctor two days earlier. Just a bad cold, he was told. "It's not the flu. Drink plenty of fluids and stay in bed."

We never discussed the idea of canceling our trip to Vegas, even though we easily could have, since we purchased optional trip insurance as we always did when we flew in winter. I don't believe it ever occurred to either one of us to stay home. We had made plans, other than work, that we really looked forward to. My brother and sister-in-law planned to meet us in Vegas as they had a couple of times in the past. Many of our greatest memories happened on those jaunts, and apparently we weren't willing to give up the opportunity to make more. We had learned, quite accidentally, that the four of us made very compatible traveling companions. My sister-in-law, Mary, insists that we discovered it because she invited them to join us on one of our first trips to Las Vegas. She maintains that the idea had initially horrified Al. I don't recall that reaction, but Al never convincingly debunked the detail.

On that initial trip, we received our Vegas names. We couldn't just pick our names. Each had to happen organically or at least have a story related to it.

Mary acquired hers first as she checked into the Las Vegas condominium they would inhabit for just one night until we could get into our timeshare the following day. She had made the reservation online and provided necessary information, but somehow the clerk at the check-in desk had her first name written as Marci. Instead of correcting the mistake, Mary accepted her new Vegas name and proclaimed it mandatory we all have one.

My brother Vern became Vince after relaying a story about his son-in-law's father who, on their first meeting, called him that for an entire weekend.

I told the story of the surprise of our hairdresser Kara when we walked into the salon for our scheduled appointment. "Oh, Chris and Al!" she shouted out. She had spent the whole day trying to figure out who Christal was, as she had written *Chris+al* in her appointment book. My Vegas name is, therefore, Crystal.

Al received his name while driving out of the west rim entrance of the Grand Canyon. We had rented a bright red minivan so we could comfortably fit four adults with luggage, but Al hated minivans and often voiced his opinion about them.

As Mary took a picture of Al behind the wheel of the vehicle, we realized that his Vegas name obviously was Van.

We acquired last names to complete the mandate in Las Vegas forevermore as Marci Oakes, Vince Vega, Crystal Palms, and Van Winkle.

Al had a difficult time grasping the concept of siblings. As an only child, he hadn't experienced the gamut of emotions, hi-jinks, and downright brawls associated with growing up with brothers and sisters—or, for instance, what it was like sharing a bedroom with two older sisters who would have the occasional sleepover party with their friends, not wanting the little sister (me), hanging around. And how they would forget about the closet in their bedroom, which abutted the closet in their brothers' bedroom and had enough space for a child to squeeze through, entering either closet at will, allowing the younger sibling to eavesdrop on the entire evening. Or how the youngest child—that again would be me—having stolen her brother's hockey stick after being told she could not use it to join her friends in a game on the local iced-over pond and getting caught by her brother as she tried to sneak the stick back into the house, thus inciting the brother to dump the milk—which he was about to pour into a glass for himself—over the head of the offending party. Again, that would be me.

As we grew older, my brother Vern and two sisters, Pam and Paula, followed their own paths. We lost the day-to-day contact we had as children and young adults. If we weren't spread across the country, we saw each other on holidays but that didn't foster personal connection.

The adults we developed into shielded us from each other as life became hectic and demanding of our time with families to raise and careers to cultivate. As I grew older, however, I realized my siblings were my first friends, rivals or not. My brother and sisters each looked out for me, the youngest of four. Since rediscovering each other, however, we have looked after each other.

I describe our evolving relationship like this:

In the beginning, we were rivals.

In the middle, we were strangers.

In the end, we are family.

I believe it bemused Al at how quickly my brother and sisters accepted him and how quickly he accepted himself as part of a larger self that also included becoming an uncle. He loved being Uncle Al. He immersed himself in the role, and he was good at it—so much so that even nieces and nephews on Mary's side of the family called him Uncle Al as well as our friends' children. His hearty laugh and enormous hugs gave him a Santa-like quality, which came in quite handy when he got asked to portray the big guy on occasion.

Al previously worked at a Marlboro start-up company, CrossCom. He loved the job and challenge of a new company, but mostly he loved the people he worked with.

One Christmastime, a co-worker asked Al if he would show up as Santa during a family gathering. Al had portrayed Santa not long before at the Mountain Barn Restaurant in Princeton, where I worked as a cook. Al gladly agreed to the co-worker's request, and I went with him to his friend's house the night of the party.

I remember three children there, one of them Marissa, his friend's daughter, about whom Al had heard stories at work.

The children each took a turn sitting on Santa's lap and getting a present from Santa, each specifically picked out and provided by the parents.

When Marissa nearly finished her talk with Santa, he said, "Merry Christmas, Marissa."

Her eyes got wide. She jumped off his lap and ran over to her parents. "Mommy," she said. "He knows my name!"

We retold of that beautiful moment over and over, especially at Christmas.

Early winter mornings in Massachusetts can be hazardous, no matter what the current weather produced. Even when the temperatures hover above freezing, roads can take on a shine, either innocently wet from dew or perilously dangerous from dreaded black ice. It had been unusually warm as we made our way along Millers River towards Route 91, and as the temperature rose, so rose the fog. Al was behind the wheel of our white Dodge Journey meandering along the winding two-lane road—at twenty miles an hour over the speed limit.

I suppose it should have occurred to me earlier, but not until we reached the first curve, contacted black ice, and glided off the road towards a six-foot ditch did I consider maybe I should be behind the wheel. The rear tires struggled to keep hold of the frozen shoulder as Al instinctively spun the wheel into an over-exaggerated left-hand turn and then a course-correcting right. As he regained control, I heard myself cursing, adamantly announcing my displeasure with his driving. I told him to pull over at the convenience store just ahead. I would drive. He didn't argue. He didn't dispute. That's when it sunk in how horrible he must have felt.

And then the first twinges of guilt set in.

I learned, early on, how to deal with guilt. How to turn it off, pack it away, and on occasion, ignore it. I've also learned that guilt and regret frequently go hand in hand. But regrets are tricky, because we usually think of them out of context based on retrospective analysis, and then know after the fact what we didn't know before. Regrets tend to linger like unwelcome fumes from a frightened skunk. But how potent and influential regrets can be and how difficult to live with the odor.

Guilt, however, is a by-product of a conscious decision, which makes it powerful, predominant, and precarious . . . like nearly ending up in a ditch because you should have made the decision to drive in the first place.

We drove in silence. Al's struggle for breath amplified.

I grew up in a Catholic household, the guardian of guilt. When we were children, our parents expected my siblings and me to fulfill the Catholic trilogy: Baptism, First Communion, and Confirmation. As an infant, I had no voice in the first. However, for the other two events, I was old enough to participate in the process.

I recall going to catechism classes, a torturous and time-consuming ritual. The few times I tried to skip out on classes, I got caught and, mirroring the fate of many uninspired Christians, punished. When I realized I had no

Pam, Paula, Chris, and Vern, from left, dress up on Jackson Street to celebrate Easter in 1965.

way to avoid the process without spending the rest of my life grounded, I decided to make it as unbearable as possible for my catechism teacher. I became the object of eye rolls from all the other kids. I asked question after question, interrupted as often as I could, and—within the boundaries of student to teacher—quizzed the validity of each lesson. I became a holy heckler.

I could never invest myself in the Church. That doesn't mean that I don't believe in God. I just don't believe in organized religion, especially one that uses guilt to keep its subjects in line. I prefer a more personalized approach to spirituality.

As my parents wished, I fulfilled my so-called duties, but I did not do it without taking advantage of a golden blackmail opportunity.

Chris celebrates First Holy Communion with her new baseball and glove.

photo by Joyce Johnson

For my First Communion, my parents forced me to wear a frilly white dress with white tights, black patent leather shoes, and a big white bow in my hair. An avid tomboy, I professed that outfit to be completely out of my ballpark, but I knew I wouldn't get to first base with my protests. So, like agent to owner, I began negotiations for a new baseball glove. I had simple demands: get me the glove, and I'll wear the getup just for the ceremony. And, as with all worthy agents, I succeeded. To my parents' dismay, I used my new glove for the first time on First Communion day as I wore the white frilly dress and tights before heading to church.

My parents had been Holy Communion partners: when they made their own First Communions in St. Anne's Church, Shrewsbury, Massachusetts, they walked down the aisle side by side as they would do again some dozen years later when they got married. A handsome young man, my father excelled in sports, and later in life, Shrewsbury High School

Chris's parents, Vernon Johnson Jr. and Joyce Kender Johnson, married in St. Anne's Church, Shrewsbury, in 1955.

inducted him into its hall of fame in three sports categories. He attended Worcester Polytechnic Institute, studied civil engineering, and played running back on WPI's 1954 undefeated football team. My mother, a beautiful woman who loved to sing, aspired to be a painter.

 My father, Vern Jr., grew up in a loving, stable home where family always came first. He remained close to his parents and two sisters all his life. My mother's upbringing went differently. She had an alcoholic father and emotionally distant mother. Her brother struggled with his own demons, and she never relayed any stories of their childhood together. Her parents divorced, her father eventually re-married, and her mother had a relationship with a man she brought over to the house on Christmas, every year, for many years. Not until he died did we find out through his obituary that he was married to someone else.

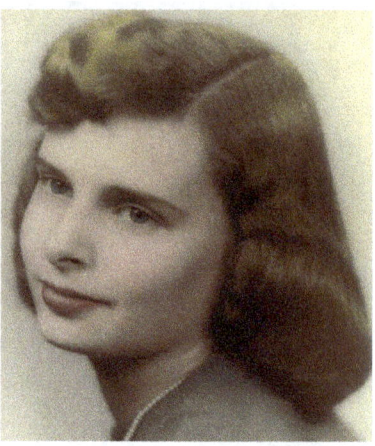

Chris's parents, Vern and Joyce, had very different upbringings.

There you have it: my grandmother showcasing her affair to us every Christmas. It wasn't her first dalliance, either. I learned later she "socialized" with at least one other married man. I never knew my mother's mother well, but I don't think she liked being a mother or a grandmother.

When I was twenty-six and working as a cook at the Mountain Barn Restaurant, my co-worker Paul badgered me to join the tenpin bowling team he and others had formed. The league had just begun, and one of the team members backed out at the last minute. They needed a fourth person to round out the team or they would have to drop out of the league. I refused multiple times, but Paul persisted, and finally, I reluctantly agreed. I hadn't bowled since my childhood Saturday morning candlepin league. I hoped Paul and his friends would need a fill-in only for the first week until they got a permanent fourth member.

Fate had a different plan.

Our opponents arrived with gear bags in hand, freshly laundered shirts with team logo and name, and confidence that swelled as they scanned our side of the mint-green bench.

He drew my attention from the moment I saw him.

Not very tall and overweight, he nevertheless carried himself with assurance both authentic and unassuming. As he laced up his bowling shoes, I noticed his hands: working hands, not chafed or dry but strong and reliable. There's something about a man's hands that I find telling and intriguing.

He reached into his bag, retrieved a blue-marbled, custom-fit bowling ball, and placed it on the ball-return rack. As he walked back to the bench, I could read his name stitched on the left front of his shirt above the pocket—Al. And as destiny would have it, I would bowl directly against him.

Before arriving to meet my other teammates, I had resigned myself to the likelihood that I would make a fool of myself and they would happily replace me the following week. And even though I am a very competitive person, I felt fine with that—until I saw Al.

I hadn't practiced, I sported well-worn rented bowling shoes, and I had chosen a ten-pound alley-owned ball, the lightest one I could find among the venue's selections. I knew how to bowl, but tenpin bowling posed a distinctly different challenge than using the smaller, lighter candlepin balls I grew up with. Candlepin balls weigh less than three pounds, and you had three chances instead of two to knock the pins down. But the concept was the same: roll the first ball between the number three and four arrows marked on the lane fifteen feet ahead of the foul line and pray that ball went straight. If it did, I wouldn't have to worry about slinging the second shot, because I'd be celebrating my perfectly thrown strike with my teammates.

He was left-handed. When he released his fifteen-pound ball, it traveled along the left gutter lip for two-thirds of the journey until the violent spin he torqued it with gripped the lane and drove it toward the pins. It fascinated me to watch. I imagined it took considerable strength to hurl.

Our opposing styles showcased the difference between a novice and a practiced participant of the sport. Because it was so obvious, I knew I had nothing to lose. And when I have nothing to lose, I can give my very best effort without stressing over the outcome, and I did exactly that. I thoroughly enjoyed the short banter we shared between each frame. I found him smart, funny, clever, and not nearly as competitive as I had imagined.

I don't recall keeping track of the score, but when we finished the first string, as improbable as it sounds, I had beaten him. He would later use the excuse that I had distracted him from the moment he saw me. He was a sweet talker. As we continued with the next two strings, the bowling universe went back on track, and our team got trounced.

The bowling alley had its own full-service bar, so with the business of bowling behind us, my teammates and I went into the bar for a few beers. Hoping to see Al among the patrons, I scanned the crowded room. I felt surprisingly disappointed when I didn't find him there. Surprising, because I wasn't looking for a man in my life. I had long before resigned myself to thinking that I wouldn't succeed at relationships, so I felt no need to pursue one. But I suspected something different this time. I felt drawn to him.

I had nearly finished my first beer when he walked into the bar and skimmed the room. I spied him instantly because I hadn't taken my eyes off the door since we sat down. He spotted me spotting him, walked past the table where his teammates gathered, and took a seat beside me. Eventually, as the room began to empty, we moved up to the bar. Never missing a beat, we talked non-stop—no uncomfortable silence or searching for the right words. We talked about our childhoods, our goals, our work, and for some reason that I can't remember, we went through each other's wallets. It was easy, it was familiar, it was thrilling, it was wonderful. At some point, we realized we were the only two left in the bar besides the incredibly patient bartender, the only one of us who wanted the night to come to an end. So Al and I sat in the parking lot, talking and listening to music until four o'clock in the morning.

Had we met during the era of cell phones and social media the following week may not have been so agonizing. We hadn't exchanged phone numbers, most likely because neither one of us spent any time at home. Because of the lack of contact during that week and my lack of confidence, I talked myself into thinking I had imagined how well we hit it off. I recall a telephone conversation with my mother as

I recounted the night's interactions and told her that I had most likely misconstrued the entire evening, that he probably hadn't thought about me at all.

Unlike the first week, my wish of a one-week engagement long forgotten, I looked forward to the arrival of the second bowling night. I got to the alley a bit early. A quick search revealed that Al hadn't arrived, so I checked the schedule on the board to see the lane assigned to my team that night. I also checked to see Al's lane. His team would bowl at the opposite end of the building, too far away for a chance run-in.

As those thoughts swirled in my head, I noticed Jane, one of Al's teammates, heading toward me. Except for the usual niceties, I hadn't really spoken to her the week before, but she greeted me like an old friend and told me that Al was at night school and would show up later that evening. She said she had strict orders not to let me leave until he got there. I feigned indifference, but all the while, my insides did a little jig. He had thought about me after all.

I had never let myself get close to anyone or let them see me—the real me—until that day in October of 1987 when I went bowling. In my few previous relationships, I found myself unable to participate actively, too unsure of myself to interject my own thoughts or emotions. Yet, on that first night with Al, I told him things I had never told anyone, intensely personal and private things.

Some might call it love at first sight, although I think that's a little melodramatic. However, we experienced something special. Something I couldn't quite explain happened the night we met. It felt as if we had known each other forever, yet I had never laid eyes on him. I felt comfortable with him from the start, yet I had never felt comfortable with any man. The feeling I had—and still have—is that we had done it all before.

My parents got divorced for the *second* time when I was thirteen, at least I understood it that way at the time. Technically, they got divorced only once, but when I was about ten, on the original day the divorce would have been final, they decided

Celebrating Easter Sunday in the mid sixties at the family restaurant— Vern's Restaurant in Sutton, named for Chris's grandfather Vern Sr.— are, from front, left, Vern 3rd, Pam, Chris, and Paula, with their parents Vern Jr. and Joyce.

to give it another try. I don't remember any of us siblings being happy, excited, or even mildly hopeful about the decision. Many reasons contributed to the collapse of their marriage, not the least of them my mother's mental state. Consequently, I spent most of my days outside away from the turmoil that filled our little house on Jackson Street. I also started to rebel around that time, push the envelope of discipline, and apparently form my views on marriage.

My life growing up was like tiptoeing through a densely populated cow pasture, trying to avoid steaming mounds of shit. No matter my diligence, how carefully I chose my path, nor how much I weighed every step, a shrouded slippery slope always propelled me into a hot fresh pile of excrement.

From the outside, our family looked normal, whatever constituted normal in those days—or today: two parents and four children living in a small three-bedroom house on a private street, a large yard perfect for playing kick-the-can, army, or hide-and-seek. One of our neighbors owned a pony, Macaroni, a small Shetland housed in a corral adjacent to our front lawn, and we sometimes fed him apples from another neighbor's tree. Those neighbors had a huge field behind their house where we played baseball, football, or just horsed around.

Normal.

It was a much simpler time, some would say, the 1960s and early 1970s. We had stay-at-home-moms, dinner at six, and had to go home when the streetlights turned on. We went from owning a black and white television to a color TV. Records turned into eight track tapes, and telephones still had

Sitting around the kitchen table on Thanksgiving, 1974, are from left, brother Vern, father Vern, Chris, and sister Paula.

cords. When not in school, we spent the entire day outside, playing with the other kids from the neighborhood until it was time for dinner, and we were not allowed to be late. We had lunch at the closest house when we got hungry, or sometimes we skipped it altogether. Wonderful childhood memories fill my head, proving that the human spirit is indomitable, protective, and to some extent deceiving.

I never thought it strange that, as a young child getting ready to go to school, I quietly ducked into my parents' bedroom where my mother still slept, grabbed lunch money from her pocketbook, and headed off to the bus stop. It never occurred to me that other mothers, already awake, made breakfast or helped their kids get dressed before school. It never occurred to me that, when they got back from school, most children found their mothers at home, where their mothers gave them snacks or asked about their day. It never occurred to me that most mothers took an interest in their children's daily life. But what occurs to me now, many years later, is that my mother paid attention when I broke the rules or behaved badly. At least then I got a reaction from her and got her attention, her wrath.

Today they call her condition bipolar disorder, but back then, they called it manic depression. We, however, didn't call it anything, because you just didn't talk about things like that, not to anyone, not even each other. Nobody did.

Growing up is hard. Children need to know what is expected of them and what the rules are and the consequences of breaking those rules. Imagine if the rules keep changing without warning. That describes our world, our little *normal* house on Jackson Street.

My mother, Joyce, loved to socialize. She could be exuberant, raucous, the life of the party. Our house became a gathering place for my parents' friends, who threw themed events such as the beatnik party in our basement. Our parents instructed us to stay upstairs and go to bed at the allotted time, but we kept the cellar door open and caught glimpses of the adults dressed in fringed suede jackets and knee-high go-go boots. Some wore wigs, and some of the men sported fake mustaches. One of the gentleman guests held a large stick of salami that he gnawed on most of the night, and if there was any significance to that, I have never discovered it. Another friend rode his son's motorcycle into the basement, filling it up with fumes to mix with cigarette smoke. Of course, my parents' parties always involved alcohol, sometimes straight from the bottle and sometimes a carefully prepared punch, but always booze.

My father acquiesced to my mother's desire for socializing, even though, I believe, he had trepidation about how the evenings might unfold. When my mother went through an extreme high, an extreme low would inevitably follow. Not until his last years did my father openly discuss the more life-altering issues he and my mother endured, although he occasionally slipped up and alluded to things he had no intention of discussing with me.

A private dirt road off Worthington Avenue, Jackson Street leads to the only house on the street, the house where I grew up. Dense wooded areas surrounded our suburban neighborhood with winding paths created by all the neighborhood kids. The paths brought us to other neighborhoods and destinations in town. We had our own well-worn, partially blazed private highway system in those woods, so we made sure to protect it.

I came home late for dinner one night when I was about ten years old and exhilarated from the day's events. A small brush fire had ignited behind a friend's house on Worthington Avenue between our neighborhood and Jordon Pond, and the fire department brought in two of their trucks to handle the situation. My friends and I desperately wanted to join in on the activity, so a firefighter handed us each a small silver cylinder with a built-in handle and a hose about three feet long with a spray nozzle sprouting from the top of the canister. The cylinders were full of water, and he told us to stay on the outskirts of the brush fire and douse remaining embers that could reignite. My, how times have changed!

How invigorating to do something so important, something I knew my parents would be proud of, something I felt so proud of. Once the cylinders depleted and the firetrucks left to go back to their stalls, I went home for supper. I smelled like one of the many ashtrays scattered throughout our house and couldn't wait to tell my story. Beaming with pride, I stepped through the kitchen door and met five pairs of eyes, one pair that seemed to shoot out enough flames to have started the brush fire.

Not only was I late for dinner, my mother screamed, but I was disgustingly dirty. And I smelled. She wouldn't let me tell my story, how heroic I had been, how I helped save the neighborhood, how I got so dirty.

She sent me to the shower. No supper for me.

By the way, as an example of the indomitable and protective human spirit, I remember the incident as a happy memory more about the thrill of helping put out the fire than about my mother's hysterical anger.

On a side note, the fire department used to let us kids ride on the back of the trucks sometimes, usually when they came to flush out hydrants. Their young cargo feeling like superheroes, smiles as bright as the sun, the trucks drove slowly down our dead-end street. Of course, such a thing could never happen today, poor kids.

Weighing our words before we spoke, trying not to interrupt her nor wake her when she slept, we learned to be cautious around my mother. The most innocent of comments could result in a violent emotional and sometimes physical outburst. I vividly remember her fingernails digging into my wrist and the back of my hand as the hard, plastic hairbrush connected with my knuckles. Some of it I probably deserved, even asked for. I could be a handful at times. I couldn't always rely on the rules that, without any prior notice, changed as quickly as my mother's moods.

Aside from instantaneous mood swings and bouts of inactivity, another symptom of manic depression concerns making bad decisions, sometimes of a sexual nature. I had learned about an incident when I was in my mid-to-late teens: her indiscretion with a man, who, with his wife, was part of my parents' larger circle of friends. I never learned nor wanted to know specifics, but I'm sure that indiscretion played a major role in the demise of my parents' marriage. I would be told, years later, that the "friend" may not have been the only indiscretion.

I recall one day, my father visibly anxious and in a hurry packing us up into the station wagon, to go look for my mother. She had left the house that day, again. Just walked away. We drove through town searching, drove to the Quinsigamond bridge, a place she had gone before, and kept driving until he could think of no other place to look.

We returned home unsuccessful, and sometime later my father received a phone call from the police. They had found my mother wandering along Lake Avenue in Worcester near Lake Quinsigamond.

The bridge seemed to call to my mother when she felt suicidal. Surely, she had other options, but that one had a hold on her, maybe because the bridge overlooked the house where she grew up.

My mother didn't choose to be that way. No one does. Over the years, science has told us that depression is a complicated disorder, most likely a combination of genetic and non-genetic factors more recently linked to serotonin levels that act as neurotransmitters in the brain. The condition isn't something that you can just "get over" or "pull yourself up from." As I understand the condition, it requires diligent monitoring of medications. In the 1960s, the lack of understanding of the illness limited her treatment. After my father dealt with escalating bouts and after consulting with her doctor, he declared my mother mentally ill and arranged for hospitalization in Worcester State Hospital, an institution that specialized in treatment of the illness.

The treatment for my mother's manic depression involved sending electric currents through her brain, an intervention called electroshock therapy. I was about seven when we went to visit her after one of the many procedures. We weren't allowed in the room, so we stood in the dank hallway behind a cold metal door with a small glass window allowing just enough of a view to see her lying catatonic in the bed, a slight bit of drool sliding down her cheek. I have that picture in my head. My sister Paula recently found a hand drawn get-well card that she made for my mother depicting the same scene.

Paula would have been about ten years old at the time. We never talked about it until recent years.

The treatments wiped out most of my mother's childhood memories, but the ghosts of the memories remained, haunting her, while she could not make sense out of them. Even so, she seemed to do well when she came home. Even the endless fights my parents once had—vicious and intense verbal altercations—became a little less frequent, at least for a while.

Then came her accident. As she drove the old green station wagon up Belmont Hill in Worcester, a drunk driver jumped the median in a truck traveling in the opposite direction and hit her head on. She was lucky to survive, initially left without medical attention by first responders who thought she had died at the scene. She would eventually recover physically, but emotionally, the accident took its toll.

She required more hospital stays, usually in the psychiatric ward, locked to prevent patients from wandering away. We visited as often as possible, sometimes taking her out for the day to go to the movies. The older we got, the less frequent the hospital stays. The doctors prescribed Diazepam, the generic drug otherwise known by the brand name Valium, also known as "mother's little helper." The medication appeared to lessen her suicidal tendencies and psychosis but not her mood swings.

We continued to keep our guards up.

Thus, our family's so-called normal. My mother struggled daily, but she didn't let it stop her from becoming an accomplished watercolor artist. After my parents divorced, she went back to college to study art, something she had wanted to do before she got married and had children. She would later tell me that, if she had it to do all over again, she would never have had kids. As terrible as it may sound to tell your daughter that you wished you had never given birth to her, I didn't take it personally, because I understood her meaning. Back in the 1950s, society expected a woman to get married and have children. My grandmother pressured my mother to follow suit, and she didn't feel she had a choice. But I did have a choice, she told me repeatedly. I could be or do whatever I wanted, she often reminded me, and she envied that.

The human spirit can overcome any obstacle if given a chance. We must seed, water, nurture, and harvest the resiliency we can all cultivate. Somehow in the early twenty-first century, however, we seem drawn more to the victim outlook than to the survive-and-thrive attitude. Wrestling as she did every day with the depression demon inside, my mother could easily have given up, but she didn't identify as victim. As a child, she had taught herself to survive. And she taught me to survive—not to dwell, not to envy, but to move ahead, to live my life on my terms.

Both of my parents encouraged me to forge my own path and do what made me happy. I will always hear my father as the practical voice in my head and experience my mother as the idealistic influence. The combination has served me well over the years, whether it be with my careers, financial decisions, or personal life.

Every summer we went camping, a great way for a family of six to travel without spending too much money. Our good friends, the Carters, usually accompanied us. They also numbered a half dozen. We started out with a tent, moved on to a tent trailer, and eventually enjoyed a little fourteen-foot hardtop about the size of the popular tiny houses of today but without any of the forward-thinking amenities, aside from the much appreciated and equally tiny bathroom. Our adventures took us to Nova Scotia, Cape Cod, Pennsylvania, and countless other east-coast destinations.

July 20, 1969: I had turned eight years old just thirteen days before as we camped near Cadillac Mountain in Maine's Arcadia National Park. A beautiful clear day framed the historical event about to take place. Scattered outside the tent trailer under the tarp, we watched the small black-and-white television we had brought with us for the occasion, the Apollo 11 moon landing. Only our family had a TV, so a large crowd of campers huddled around the set.

That day, you could see the moon in the daylight sky, and we found ourselves frequently looking up at it. In fact, at one point, one of the onlookers purported to seeing the Eagle spacecraft on the moon with her naked eyes. Of course, it was impossible, but the great hype expanded imaginations. We watched at 3:17 in the afternoon, Eastern Standard Time, as the lunar module softly touched down on the surface like a feather wafting to the ground. Six and a half hours later, we would hear Neil Armstrong utter those famous words,

photo by Joyce Johnson

We hung blankets to block the sun from a small television set as we viewed the Apollo 11 moon landing in July, 1969 during a camping trip to Arcadia National Park, Maine, with family and friends including, from left, front, Joey Carter, Marcelle Carter, Joe Carter, and Chris's dad, Vern; back, Chris, her brother Vern and sister Pam, Claudia Carter, Jimmy Carter, Karen Carter, and Chris's sister Paula.

"That's one small step for a man, one giant leap for mankind." We shared an exciting time in history and an especially memorable trip because of it.

With her camera always at the ready, my mother documented every trip with hundreds of pictures—physical, not digital, in those days—including the moon landing, which she had developed into slides. I remember her trying to get us to pose in front of a large sign that could have been anywhere: there was always a large sign that said, "Entering . . . " or "Welcome to . . . ." All of us kids griped, but it didn't help. She never let a photo opportunity pass her by, and she could never take a photo without a perfectly placed foreground subject—a flower, tree or something else to help frame the scene. The endeavor resembled asking a pack of puppies to sit still while you paint the Mona Lisa.

After my mother passed away, we spent many retrospective days viewing thousands of slides and choosing the ones we would store electronically and the ones we would cast away. The disproportionate piles produced the larger stack as evidence of happy times, times we could let our guard down for a short while, the calm before the inevitable storm.

When the boys reached their teenage years and therefore old enough to play in summer Little League, we couldn't leave to go camping. My mother came up with a solution. We transformed our yard into a campground for our family, friends, and neighbors for two weeks in July. Our parents put the house off limits to all campers for all reasons other than emergencies. It's interesting what some people decided constitutes an emergency. At any given time, we had from five to seven campsites in our yard, some of us in tents, the lucky ones in hardtops. We called it Camp Calamity because when my mother told us about the idea, we were watching the movie, *Calamity Jane*. We repurposed a piece of wood paneling from our basement and painted the newly established name on the back side. Some campers traveled from a few miles away, others from next door.

The adults came up with a schedule with each of them responsible for some sort of activity, whether cooking dinner one night or organizing game day for us kids. Every year, my mother arranged for our local priest, Father James F. Hoey,

The families Carter, Williams, and Johnson set up Camp Calamity.

to say an outdoor mass one of the evenings. We created an improvised altar and added outdoor lighting to give it a festive look. The lights also attracted mosquitoes. One night during mass as Father Hoey read from his bible, the bugs became too much for him to bear, so he asked the altar boy for bug spray. He sprayed the Holy Bible first, layering a thick, heavily scented foam onto the sacred book. The result horrified him, and he quickly wiped the foam off with the dangling sleeve of his robe. He shot an unpleasant glance at the boy who handed him the can. Apparently, the boy hadn't read the label, which indicated that the stuff wasn't aerosol.

When Father Hoey came to deliver the outdoor mass on a separate occasion, he had agreed to stay and camp overnight in a one-person pup tent. I'm sure my mother sold him on the idea of general camaraderie and singing around the campfire.

If he could have found a way to back out gracefully, I believe he would have.

It had rained all day and continued throughout the evening. He said mass under cover, so we managed well, but because of the weather, everyone went to bed early, so no camaraderie and no singing around the campfire.

In the morning, Father Hoey emerged from his water-logged tent with puffy red eyes and a rash covering his face, arms, and only he knew where else. He revealed that he had not slept alone that night. Every ant within walking distance had visited his easily accessible tent, staked directly to the ground. I'm unsure how the rash occurred, but so much for his potentially pleasant stay.

I also remember a four-year-old neighbor boy camper who picked a crabapple from the ground under our tree, put it in a plastic beach bucket, and, hoping to grow a full-sized apple, covered it with water. Two days later, sometime during the night while the child slept, my mother conspired with other mothers and replaced the crabapple with a beautiful, fully ripe apple from the neighbor's tree. The boy was thrilled to find it the next morning and showed it off to everyone.

Food always played an integral part in Camp Calamity. When we traveled to camp, we usually kept our food pretty basic: hot dogs, hamburgers, and sandwiches, but at Camp Calamity we ventured out more, probably because we saved money on travel and could afford a little bit of food luxury. One late afternoon, the campers decided that every family would chip in money and order Chinese food from our favorite place in Westborough. Somehow, the camping powers that be decided the moment constituted an emergency, so they allowed my brother, Vern 3rd, to go into the house and use the telephone to place the order for pickup. If the Chinese man who took the order hadn't told my brother, "You bring big truck," we would have ended up with 127 pupu platters when we really wanted only seven along with a long list of other food items. Somehow, the man misunderstood my brother or my brother misunderstood the man, but luckily, they caught the mistake in time.

My grandparents, my father's parents, owned a restaurant in Sutton, Massachusetts, called Vern's Restaurant, named after my grandfather, Vern Sr. One day they surprised everyone when they showed up with a bushel each of lobsters and steamers they brought from the restaurant. Along with the fresh corn on the cob and coleslaw they packed, it made for a huge treat and indulgence that we all devoured.

However, as a very competitive tomboy, I liked game day best. We had relay races, an egg toss, contests of all sorts, and games that didn't have names. But it wouldn't have been complete without freshly made fried bread dough covered with powdered sugar, maple syrup, cinnamon-sugar, or just plain butter, a favorite of the kids and adults alike.

Lots more happened over the years at our homemade campground. I can't recall if we held Camp Calamity for three summers or four, but it provided us with lasting memories, nice memories that stand out. When Mom was not herself

Camp Calamity entertained families for two weeks during several summers.

calamitous, she could create a fun and happy environment for us, thus alleviating the impact of the stressful times.

I drove cautiously on the highway to Windsor Locks, Connecticut, and Bradley International Airport for our flight to Las Vegas. Headlights of oncoming vehicles made it difficult for me to see due to my astigmatism, which causes light to distribute unevenly on my retinas, one of the reasons Al always drove when it was dark. Fortunately, I had an easy and uneventful drive to the airport. I still felt guilty that I hadn't offered to drive from the moment we left the house.

I had hoped Al would sleep on the ride, and he did try, but didn't succeed. He was sweat-sodden and extremely exhausted.

I parked the car in the airport's Number 4 long-term lot where we usually parked. The airport shuttle pulled up just as we unloaded our bags. I remember feeling grateful for their quick arrival. Al didn't need to stand outside on that drizzly morning.

The shuttle took us directly to the Delta terminal where we printed our boarding passes from one of many unoccupied kiosks, one of the advantages of booking the first flight of the day. We had a brief burst of elation when we saw we were eligible for the Transportation Security Administration Pre-Check line. Pre-Check felt like hitting the TSA lottery. Not only do you go through a shorter line, but you don't have to get half undressed before going through the metal detector, which that day offered a great relief.

Once through the security process, we asked an attendant for a wheelchair. Al had been on his feet for a while by then and wasn't up to walking the length of the building, with our boarding gate at the furthest end of the terminal. We'd previously played out the scenario with a wheelchair. Last time, I used one on our way to Louisville as I recovered from breaking my leg. But Al was also very familiar with wheelchairs.

Waiting for the chair to arrive, we sat on a white plastic bench just outside the security area.

I moved in with my father around 1982 after my grandfather sold his restaurant, where I had worked and lived. My father and I both assumed I would live temporarily with him, and I did, if you consider seven years temporary. I wasn't the only sibling seeking shelter at my dad's house. Vern, Mary, and their two kids moved in when I did, since we had lived together at the restaurant.

Dad became accustomed to housing his children. As adults, we all lived with him at some point.

In late October 1987, I waited for Al to pick me up in his maroon four-wheel-drive pickup truck to go on our first official date. Paul and his girlfriend Becky had invited us to play cards and have a few drinks at their apartment in Rutland.

It misted on that cold evening that turned out just a bit warmer than previous days when rain and snow accumulated at the bottom of my father's sloped driveway and froze in front of the garage door.

Nervous and excited about our date, I watched from the kitchen. My stomach did a flip when I saw his truck headlights as he pulled into the driveway. I hurried out the kitchen door to the garage to let him in. I expected to see his incredibly engaging smile through the garage-door window, but . . . nothing.

I began to wonder if he had changed his mind. Seeing nothing but darkness ahead, I shifted my gaze downward. There he was in spread formation on his stomach with his head cupped in both hands. His twinkling blue eyes stared up at me with that amazing smile I had been waiting for.

I suppose I should have asked if he were alright, but instead I went into a nervous laughing fit.

Sore with nothing broken, he explained how black ice in the driveway caused him to slide toward the door before he hit the puddle of ice and fell. He didn't have time to recover his footing, so he struck the pose just as I opened the door.

I thought he was adorable. It turns out Al had plenty of experience falling. I would see him laid out on the floor or ground plenty of times in the future.

It was the third Monday in April. I remember because I had been listening to the Boston Marathon on the car radio, and the marathon always takes place on Patriots Day, a Maine and Massachusetts holiday since 1894 and observed since 1969 on the third Monday in April. The holiday commemorates the battles of Lexington and Concord and of Menotomy in 1775. Many know the Lexington and Concord story, but Menotomy, not so much. As the story goes, the British retreated from Concord and headed back into Boston through Menotomy, renamed Arlington in 1867. There, five thousand patriots greeted them, and they became the first British troops to surrender.

Patriots Day also meant a day off from work for some but not all. Al got it off, but I had to work. The meteorologists had forecast a nice day, so Al decided that he would stain shingles on the back side of our deck. I told him I would try to make it a short day so I could get home before dark to help. I worked in food service sales at the time, so I could tweak my schedule as necessary. I asked him not to get up on the ladder until I got home, but I might as well have asked a child not to touch poison ivy.

I got the phone call around mid-afternoon. The ladder had buckled beneath him as he stretched the limits of its capabilities. He had plummeted to meet the concrete pad below, the heel of his right foot constituting the first casualty. If not for our neighbor walking her dog, Al may have lain in the back yard for hours.

I wanted to call an ambulance, but Al insisted he could get into the car if I brought it closer. I retrieved a chair from the kitchen, and the neighbor and I managed to lift him onto it so he could slide into the front seat.

Miraculously, immediate damage was contained to his leg. X-rays showed a compound fracture in his tibia and fibula and a shattered ankle, the bone reduced to slivers. Surgeons could fix his lower leg with rods and pins that the doctors planned to keep in permanently. The ankle itself proved more complicated. The surgeon needed to gather up the bone fragments and mill them into a powder, producing a paste. He sculpted Al's ankle back together so that his own bone material would propagate with anything left intact. For six months, he couldn't put any weight on it. He spent his recovery in a living room recliner with a stocked cooler on the floor and a walker to assist him in getting to the bathroom. As luck would have it, our dog, an English pointer named Casey, had just undergone surgery on her leg and recovered along with him. I put her next to the recliner in a child's playpen so they could keep each other company.

Al would never live another day without pain. Early on in his recovery, doctors prescribed painkillers to help him manage, but as time progressed, he set that medication aside and instead gobbled up ibuprofen like Chiclets. He underwent a couple more surgeries, one to remove the rods and pins because they created healing issues and caused pain, another to fuse his ankle so it wouldn't bend, since his arthritis had grown unbearable. The injury to his leg eventually wreaked havoc in his hips and on his back, limiting his abilities, which saddened and frustrated him greatly.

If I could go back to one day in this lifetime and change one thing, it would be that day, that outcome, that decision to touch the poison ivy. But we can't put the lead ball back into the musket once it's fired. Actions reap consequences, and that one would impact us greatly for the rest of his life.

Almost two years after we met at the bowling alley, we got married atop Mount Wachusett in Princeton. I think we both knew early on that we would marry, although decidedly it formed an unexpected event for me, since I had thought I'd never marry.

While planning the wedding, we opted to keep it simple and relatively small: a twenty-minute ceremony performed by a justice of the peace followed by a barbecue for a hundred guests outside the lodge at the base of the mountain. We splurged on a live band, or I should say, Al's parents splurged on the band. My father paid for the meal for all in attendance.

We set the date for August 7, a perfect complement to our already symbiotic birthdays, June 7 and July 7, thus initiating use of the familiar phrase *yours, mine, and ours*.

My godfather, Uncle Bill, voiced a small issue with the scenario when he adamantly asked, "Who the hell gets married on a Monday?"

We do!

We chose a Monday for other reasons. I worked four days a week, ten-to-twelve-hour days. Our honeymoon could last longer if we scheduled the wedding on a Monday, and I would have to use only one of my two weeks allotted vacation time. Al had more time off from his job, so we didn't have to take that into account.

Another benefit of throwing a wedding on a Monday? We could hire any band, caterer, or venue without conflict.

Hoping to catch the beginning of the sunset from the top of the mountain, we set a six o'clock ceremony that would also minimize the time our guests would have to take off on a typical work day.

The morning of the big day arrived, and my father's house filled with my mother, sisters, friends, a hairdresser, and Al's friend Eddie, the photographer. Preparations commenced as Eddie snapped away. He had taken the gig as a favor, so I had to restrain myself from snapping back at him, since he seemed to be everywhere. I have never enjoyed having my picture taken, so I probably made things difficult for Eddie.

Al spent the bulk of the day fishing with his best man, Dave. It had barely reached mid-morning before I wished myself on the boat with them.

Sunshine had been forecast for the day with clouds and rain moving in during late afternoon. We kept a close eye on radar reports and, as infrequently happens, the meteorologists got it spot on. We had a contingency plan to move the wedding reception inside if necessary, so we made the call early that day. We cut it close for the ceremony itself, since we had no cover should the weather turn sour.

Halfway through the twenty-minute ceremony, the skies opened up, and so did the umbrellas. I looked over to see my dad handing out golf umbrellas from the trunk of his car as the unmistakable *thwop, thwop, thwop* of them opening resonated from the onlookers.

One of the umbrellas made its way over our heads as the justice of the peace asked, "Should I continue?"

Hell, yes, I thought. *Just pick up the pace a bit.*

"Yes, please," we actually said.

Other than the band, Al and I left our wedding last. Our guests seemed to have a great time, especially those drinking champagne from Chip's cowboy boot and Becky's red pumps. The lodge manager told us that party-goers had exhausted its supply of champagne.

It rained from the middle of our vows till the end, but it never dampened our day. Someone mentioned that rain on a wedding day means good luck.

It certainly poured good fortune on us.

Chris's father Vern, left, and mother Joyce, right, flank Chris and Al at their 1989 wedding.

Al's laugh could carry a room. He had a deep, barrel-chested, contagious laugh that still echoes in my head. Confident and stout, lovable and kind, nurturing and considerate, he did little things that made him so extraordinary. He often put gas in my car because he knew I hated to stop at the station and did the laundry I detested or bought me the book I had mentioned sometime the week before. But everyone remembers him best for his hugs that wrapped you in irresistible warmth and devoured you as he held on just a little longer than anticipated, the sincerity of his embrace enhanced. A bad day could melt away with just one of his hugs.

Not a day went by without him telling me he loved me, something I was unaccustomed to hearing until he came into my life. Before leaving for work in the morning, he woke me up, looked at me with his brilliant blue eyes, and told me he loved me. Just by the example of his actions, he taught me about real, unconditional love and how to express it. What better lesson to teach someone?

He was also adventurous, a fact corroborated by his bucket list. He wanted to fly fish in New Zealand, explore Alaska, and learn how to fly an airplane, all of which went undone for reasons that seem inconsequential now. That's not to say he didn't get to cross some major things off his list. He hunted antelope in Wyoming and bear in North Carolina. He owned the motorcycle his mother never wanted him to have. However, his list became less feasible once the ladder buckled beneath him.

Al scores an antelope in Wyoming in autumn, 2012.

After his accident, he lost a bit of his spark. He knew he could never hike the Rockies to chase elk or comfortably wade through a salmon-filled Idaho river. It didn't stop him, but knowing the limit of possibilities gave him great sorrow. His ideas of adventure would have to change.

We had spoken many times about owning our own business, independent of corporate buyouts and layoffs. More than once, Al had fallen victim to such circumstances that created uncertainty and instability in our financial situation and stress in our personal arena. We had both assumed, when the time came, we would open a restaurant, utilizing my culinary and organizational skills and Al's managerial and business skills. But we don't always choose our path. Often our path chooses us.

We had been shooting sporting clays for almost ten years before we attempted the US Open. We began at our local gun club, a nice course open once a week on Sunday mornings. A friend invited Al and me to accompany him on guest day. Al had his own twelve-gauge hunting shotgun, but I didn't own one, so I shared a lightweight twenty-gauge gun with one of the gracious gun club members.

Most people mistakenly think of sporting clays as trap shooting, which uses one clay target machine housed sixteen yards in front of the shooting positions and sending clay discs away from the shooters, who move in a semi-circle behind the machine. But the challenge of sporting clays is best described as "golf with a shotgun," because participants play it on a large course, usually in a wooded area, and participants move from station to station just like golfers move to the next tee on a golf course once the hole is played out. Sporting clays requires many machines of different types at different stations. Machines throw varying targets with an abundance of options including going away from the shooter, crossing trajectories, incoming, or straight up in the air. Other popular targets called rabbit targets bounce along the ground.

Inventors of the game wanted to simulate hunting birds and small game. A fun game on its own whether one intends to hunt or not, shooting clays offers a great way to practice for those seasons.

I first shot rabbit targets. The person in control of the machine waited for my signal and pushed the button as I called "Pull". The disc screamed off the arm of the machine and bounced along the unevenness of the ground. As instructed, I followed the target with the muzzle of the gun and pulled the trigger. Immediately, another target came careening out of the machine. I repeated the motion and pulled the trigger a second time, the presentation known as a following pair. To my surprise, I crushed both clays and produced two bright orange bursts of powder. I was hooked. Al and I bought shotguns appropriate for target shooting and began shooting clays every Sunday morning. Eventually, we branched out to shoot at other clubs and compete in tournaments throughout the East Coast.

We once spent a week at M&M Hunting and Sporting Clays Club in New Jersey. It rained all week. We planned to arrive early in the week so we could practice during our first and only trip to the National Sporting Clays Association US Open. We wanted to make the best of it despite the rain, which made it uncomfortable and more difficult to stay focused. It cost us a fortune, but it meant another bucket item off the list. The massive place hosted as many as five full-size clays courses, multiple five-stand courses, and many other clay shooting games.

M&M also raises ducks—lots and lots of ducks.

With well over a thousand shooters attending in hundreds of vehicles, you can imagine what the soggy parking lots looked like after days of rain. The club has a special area to park the trailers used to tow our golf carts. Al and I joined up with the New England contingent there and created our own tent city. Everyone chipped in money for groceries, and we set up a few grills so we could eat at any time of day or night.

The tournament required staggered start times for competitors since not everyone could fit on the course at the same time, so we prepared and cooked food throughout the day. The tents protected us from the constant rain but not from water building up on the ground. Tire tracks from vehicles driving on the rain-soaked field created a maze of deep channels that quickly filled up with water. They presented a unique opportunity for ducks to paddle from tent to tent, visiting with all the makeshift outdoor kitchens to see what delicacy someone would toss them.

Life really is a matter of perspective, isn't it? We cursed the rain while the ducks relished it. After about three days, we noticed that one of the ducks made a small nest and laid her eggs behind the tire of a friend's trailer. It presented quite a challenge at the end of the week when our friend managed to extricate the trailer exceedingly carefully, without disturbing the eggs.

Al won a trophy at that 2005 US Open Sporting Clay Championship, something that gave him great pride. We had both previously won trophies, but that one stood out. Sporting clays became a passion of ours—a passion that would soon become our business.

Clubs often charged steep tournament entry fees, so to support our shooting habit, at larger tournaments we began selling products specific to shooting sports. We became a well-known sponsor and vendor. After a few years, our home became a warehouse overflowing with boxes, packing materials, and a large commercial embroidery machine for custom shirts and shooting vests sat in the middle of our family room.

We had to do something, and so began a new kind of adventure.

We purchased a building less than three miles from our house on the main road going through town. Since we had a building larger than we needed for storage, we decided we would open a store and sell the same products we sold on the road. Certainly a bold move, but we welcomed the challenge.

The inconspicuous steel building had previously housed a machine shop. Some would call the place ugly, but I thought of it as a blank canvas just waiting for the artist's brush to transform it into a custom piece. It took a full year to convert the interior from an uninviting metal shell into a welcoming lodge design. We indulged in an extravagance, the natural-stained tongue-and-groove pine ceiling that gave us the character we wished to project. Unfortunately, we couldn't do much with the exterior. Hoping to convey that our business concerned outdoor sporting goods, we commissioned and applied life-sized metal silhouettes of animals including deer, bears, and moose to the outside of the nondescript metal siding. As much as we prided ourselves on the inside of the store, the outside once prominently featured as the cover photo for an online blog that depicted Orange as the number one redneck town in Massachusetts.

We took that as a compliment.

We named the business Grrr Gear, with three *r*s because two *r*s weren't enough and four *r*s were too many. How the name Grrr originally came about requires a long story and possibly another book. Let's just call it an inside joke between our shooting coach and us. However, once we started using the name, people remembered it and they usually smiled when saying it, so we kept it. We opened the doors with part-time evening hours, both of us keeping our day jobs for a short time. Only a month or so later, I left my job in food-service sales and opened the store full-time, six days a week. Al continued to work his day job and joined me in the store at the end of his work day and all day on Saturdays.

Over time, we found our niche—and not with products for the competitive shooter. Our area richly favors outdoor activities, so our products reflected the strengths of the region. Once we began selling products for hunting, archery, fishing, and self-defense, our sales revealed we had hit our target audience. We continued with custom embroidery, broadening our market to create custom items for local businesses, clubs, and schools.

Although the business provided a whole new learning curve for me, Al already knew the products. Unfortunately, he had to keep working outside the store for us to pay the bills, and day-to-day running of the business fell to me.

Owning a business is not for the faint-of-heart. Creating and maintaining the store took over our lives. Every day, we experienced stress- uncertain, exhausting, and most satisfying when it ended in success or disheartening when it did not. And we felt it as the exact challenge or, dare I say, adventure we had hoped. Ironically, however, once we opened the store, we no longer had time to shoot sporting clays, thus ending our foray into competitive shooting sports.

The Bradley Airport attendant arrived with the wheelchair and proceeded at a breakneck speed to our Delta departure gate. Incapable of keeping her pace and knowing we had plenty of time, I fell behind. The terminal clock read 4:30 AM. We had made really good time due mainly to the lack of traffic at that early hour, but even so, people had already started to gather in the waiting area, the seats filling quickly. Seated near a window overlooking the aircraft we would soon board, we tried to catch a nap, but the endeavor proved fruitless.
I felt confident that, once we boarded the plane, we both could sleep. We sat in near silence as through the window we watched the day wake up.

The plane's crew gathered by the gate, the pilot standing tall with a friendly face and nice smile. I remember thinking he looked like someone with whom you could fall into a great conversation.

We would board soon according to standard practice with those needing assistance among the first in line so they have an easier time getting situated. I appreciated that because it also accorded us the benefit of not having to deal with the inevitable panic we might see on some peoples' faces as they seemed to pray that we wouldn't sit next to them. Such people evidently see being overweight as a weakness of character, and no matter how self-assured at every other moment of the day, for that single moment, I become the fat kid in gym class who couldn't climb the rope (even though it happens that, as a not particularly overweight kid, I could climb the rope). The stigma eats at my self-esteem, chews up my self-respect, and spits out my confidence, but only for a moment.

Having booked business-class tickets for the trip to Atlanta en route to Las Vegas, we would be on the side of the airplane with two seats side-by-side, no dreaded middle seat, roomier than coach, and with extra leg room. Not quite the first-class treatment we looked forward to on the leg from Atlanta to Vegas but comfortable just the same.

By then the boarding gate teemed with early morning travelers, so we knew the flight would be full. Presumably preparing the aircraft for our flight, the crew had descended the ramp when the same woman arrived to help Al onto the plane. She rolled him down the jetway to the door where the attendants stood, pleasant and dutiful. Al's joints had grown stiff after he sat for so long that the leg with all the hardware began to swell, as it had often done. He hobbled his way onto the plane and to his window seat, and I followed.

We felt relief at settling in. I realized then how much more difficult the journey had been for Al, more than I had anticipated. He was drained.

My phone read 5:15 AM.

We didn't do all our traveling by air. We discovered early in our relationship that as young adults we had both wanted a motorcycle. My mother always discouraged if not outright forbade me from getting one. She didn't think it appropriate for a girl to ride one. Possibly she saw me as so much a tomboy that my riding a motorcycle would put her over the edge. Al's mother, on the other hand, had a solid reason for not allowing him to get one. A nurse, she had seen firsthand what happens when a motorcycle literally meets the road. Al had promised his mother that, as long as she lived, he would not get one, and he honored the promise. She passed away shortly after she retired, well before Al's fortieth birthday.

When we grew up in Shrewsbury, some of the neighborhood boys, including my brother, Vern, had dirt bikes. I watched him on his sleek yellow Honda SL-70 and imagined myself in his place, careening back and forth at full throttle up the private dirt road where we lived. We had the network of neighborhoods in the woods connected by paths that would take us almost anywhere in town we wanted to go. Most of us used the paths to walk or ride our bicycles, but in my mind, the select few who had dirt bikes had it made. I watched enviously as they bounded like Evil Knievel over a mound on the ground that sent them soaring into the air, suspended for what seemed like an eternity, only to bounce back to the dirt where the nubs of the tires gripped the earth and propelled them forward—the embellished memories of a child, never forgotten, never abandoned.

On an excruciatingly hot July weekend, Al and I took the three-day motorcycle safety course sponsored by the Central Massachusetts Safety Councils in Worcester. The classroom part of the course didn't bother us; we had air conditioning. We completed riding instruction in a hot, paved parking lot devoid of trees and shade where we wore helmets, gloves, glasses, long pants (no shorts allowed), boots, and jackets—but first we would need to purchase these items.

We knew of a motorcycle shop, Cycle Design, just twenty minutes from our house so we decided to scope it out. While looking for equipment required for the class, Al fell in love with a black and yellow 650cc Honda Shadow displayed prominently just inside the front door. He wouldn't turn forty for months, but I began to form my scheme as soon as I saw the bike. We left the shop without buying anything but with a good sense of what we wanted and planned to return.

The following Friday, I went back into Cycle Design alone to talk to the owner. We developed a workable strategy where I would stop in every Friday and give her money toward purchase of the coveted Honda. We agreed that I would finance whatever balance remained as we approached the birthday deadline. She put a SOLD sign on the bike and promised to keep my secret when Al and I revisited the store to purchase our riding equipment for the class. It meant getting all her employees to cooperate as well, to pretend they didn't know me even though we had formed a fun and friendly bond. It worked perfectly, and Al was nearly heartbroken when he saw the SOLD sign. I was delighted. I financed the remainder of the balance for the Honda a week before his birthday and made plans for its delivery.

The gambit constituted by far the most elaborate birthday conspiracy I ever hatched. We scheduled his party on Saturday, so I made arrangements for delivery of his motorcycle to my neighbors' house on Friday. They would keep it covered in their yard. With the party in progress, I would have someone sneak the bike onto our front lawn and cover it with a tarp.

I got all our friends on board with the plan.

Slowly driving by our neighbors' house on Friday, I grinned at the bulky item under a blue tarp in their yard. After many covert months, I had done it. It would be the best birthday surprise ever.

As I entered the house through the kitchen door, Al stunned me as he asked from the living room, "Honey, did you buy me a motorcycle?"

His question left me momentarily speechless. I searched my brain, hoping for a plausible scenario involving a simple wild guess on his part. But then I saw it, laid out on the kitchen table: the letterhead with that unmistakable Honda logo. A package had arrived that day, in his name, with a thank you letter and warranty information ever so efficiently processed by the company.

To make it easier for registration purposes, I had filled out the paperwork in his name so the title would reflect his information. It was my turn to be heartbroken.

So the party went on as planned with the only surprise concerning which motorcycle had I bought him, which I

With assistance from Chris, right, Al unwraps his birthday "surprise."

milked for as long as I could, playfully punishing him for learning my plot. In retrospect, I suppose he had that all figured out, but ever the good sport, he feigned surprise in front of our guests.

Ever the good sport, Al feigns surprise about his birthday present.

Once in his seat, Al's wheezy and labored breathing seemed to improve. I could tell passengers filled up seats around us, but it didn't stop me from falling into a state between consciousness and sleep. I'm pretty sure Al did the same.

I had texted my brother just before boarding the plane to tell him we were on schedule. He texted back that they were just leaving their house in Warren, Massachusetts, headed to Bradley Airport, and they would meet us in the Vegas McCarren International Airport baggage claim area as planned. We traveled separately even though they only lived an hour away from us. They had booked their trip after we made our reservations—nothing unusual. We had done the same thing before. We would arrive first, pick up the rental car, and drive back to the terminal to meet them at the baggage carousel.

I drifted off.

Al shrieked a loud, piercing, non-stop shrill I had never imagined his male-dominant ego would ever allow him to utter. Vern and Mary heard him, too, from inside the Sahara Hotel and Casino where they waited for us by the roller coaster dismount area.

Al had never been a fan of roller coasters or any other amusement park ride. To this day I don't know why he agreed to go on that one. Maybe the iconic location persuaded him, but when he said he would go on *Speed-The Ride*, I jumped at the chance. The only two in line, we got seated by the attendant in the front car. He pulled the heavy foam-covered bars down over our heads to press us against the seat. We sat for what seemed an eternity that built up suspense, not the best situation for Al. As he opened his mouth to ask "When . . . ," we shot almost instantaneously from zero to forty-five miles an hour out of the building. It took our breath away—probably a good thing, as Al would have used it only to scream.

We couldn't see the whole route of the roller coaster from the starting point inside the building, but we had seen the ninety-two-foot vertical loop alongside the Las Vegas strip earlier in the day, and that had Al worried. Little did he know that the loop simply distracted from the main attraction. Seconds later, just as Al regained his ability to holler, we reached the loop that inverted us for no more than a split second. Another twenty-five mile an hour surge had us traveling at the

Chris and Al experience "Speed—the Ride" at the Sahara in Las Vegas.

speed of WOW as we twisted and turned, our bodies pulsating to the rhythm of the coaster car until we found ourselves looking straight up into the Vegas sky at a ninety-degree angle to earth, the tracks in front of us glistening from rays of sun until . . . no more track. As we sat like astronauts suspended in midair during liftoff with nothing but the moon in our sights, it sunk in what would happen next.

Just as Al processed the situation, I looked into his eyes and saw abject fear. We began the trip backwards, and the piercing shrill escaped. It persisted through the circuitous route, around the loop, and back into the casino where Vern and Mary waited, laughing. The ride lasted only forty-five seconds, but it took its toll on Al. Trying to help him out of the car, the attendant directed him to the right, the debarking side, but Al was so rattled he couldn't follow the simplest of instructions. After three attempts to exit left and the attendant repeating himself in ever increasing volume to exit to the right, we managed to get Al off the ride and to the nearest cocktail.

Mary and I stopped into the restroom on the way to the bar. By the time we got to our stools, Vern and Al were licking the bottom of their shot glasses, lapping every drop that escaped their initial swig. After chastising them for drinking without us, Mary and I got our first taste of Tuaca, an Italian liqueur with a sweet vanilla and almond essence. The bartender kept it in the refrigerator, served it in a frosted shot glass and highly recommended it. We stayed there for several hours, laughing, drinking, teasing Al and raising our glasses, shouting "Tuaca." There was a photo booth in the room, the kind you would find at a carnival or fair. Giggling like schoolchildren, and trying not to pull a muscle, we clumsily squeezed our four adult-sized bodies into the tiny booth. The strip of photos from that playful spontaneous silliness is one of my favorite keepsakes. I am unable to accurately detail the events of the rest of the day, partly because of the Tuaca, but mostly because it was filled with so many amazing, yet ordinary activities which were executed with extraordinary flair. We ate, we drank, we laughed, we loved. How do you describe one of the best days in your life? It's not about the things we did, the people we met or the food we ate, but the feeling we had, the pure joy of being together, the entirety of the emotions. The laughter still rings in my ears. How lucky I am to have these memories from our first, and number one, declared happy place.

Mary, Vern, Al, and Chris wind down in a NASCAR photo booth.

We were in the air; I vaguely remembered the takeoff process. I heard Al's voice break through my sleepy fog. He needed to use the restroom. Slightly annoyed and without uttering a word, I got up and moved into the aisle to let him out. He walked to the front of the airplane, through first class, and entered the lavatory. I reasoned that I would have to wait for him to come back before I could sleep again. My heavy lids closed.

My father had passed away six months earlier. A kind, unselfish, and honorable man completely devoted to his family, he was a planner both financially and personally, a provider, a teacher, a shelter from the storm, and the only stable adult influence I had in my life as I grew up. He loved his work as a civil engineer, and he did it very well.

My father was also quite compassionate. One day in my teens, I went with him to check on the progress of an industrial building site he had designed. After his workday ended, he told me he wanted to show me something. We drove through the massive, newly paved parking lot and stopped next to one of the few clusters of trees still standing, surrounded by a shiny black asphalt island, fresh sealant glistening in sunlight, and freshly planted grass at the base of the old trunks. He told of first walking the property, then abundantly wooded and secluded.

As he surveyed the building site, he came upon a tree, he said, and he pointed to the lonely cluster. I got out of the car to look at it, the gray bark showing signs of age and resilience.

As I circled the tree, I noticed the crude carving of a heart with two sets of initials and a plus sign between them.

I asked my father if he knew who the initials belonged to.

"No," he said, "but they must have meant a lot to someone."

So, he saved the tree from the bulldozers. He didn't know the people or if they would ever come back to that spot to see if their carving still stood, but that didn't matter. He felt the need to save it.

That was Dad.

He battled several forms of cancer before he died. I never heard him complain, and he never missed a family function in all that time.

For a select few, my father told the story of how he met Al. It usually embarrassed me when he did, and I tended to blush.

Chris and Al enjoy time at her dad's in 1987.

You see, they met one morning over coffee as, intending to leave for work, Al left my bedroom and went downstairs.

My father sat in the kitchen with his coffee and newspaper. Al introduced himself and sat down. They spent the next hour or so getting to know one another. Their morning chat quickly became routine and, sometime later, Al told me that he considered it the best part of his day.

At Dad's insistence, we lived with him for almost two years until we got married, thus saving money to buy our house.

For Al, my father represented the father Al wished he had. The relationship with his own father was strained at best. Many reasons accounted for the situation, Al told me, and the most outstanding concerned trade school.

Al looked forward eagerly to beginning high school classes at the new trade school in Marlborough. With a passion for race cars and adept at fixing and building things, Al enrolled in auto mechanics. When he arrived at school in September, administrators assigned him to an electronics program. Al pointed out the error, and the authorities told him that, during the summer, his father changed his subject of study. They said it was too late to change it back.

Al was furious. His father nevertheless insisted he stay in electronics, his father's own field, and insisted it would make a better profession. Al spent the rest of his life in a bittersweet career in electronics: very successful yet full of animosity and fury. He became disengaged from his father, making it extremely difficult when, years later, we both agreed his father could not take care of himself and would have to move in with us.

After Al's mom passed away in 1993, his father got into the habit of driving their small motor home to Orange from Marlboro to camp in our driveway. We installed a cable connection for him to hook up so he could watch the Red Sox, Patriots, and Bruins games in the RV.

I worked weekends, so I didn't mind at the time. Al interacted with him more than I did. He eventually increased the number of his trips, and for two years, his father showed up at our house every weekend. When winter weather prohibited use of the motor home, Al picked him up in Marlboro on Friday nights and brought him back on Monday mornings on his way to work.

I left the restaurant business in the 1990s during those two years and took a sales position with Acme Pre-Pak in Worcester. Several reasons occasioned the move, but mostly Al and I looked forward to having weekends off together, something we hadn't had since we met.

His father's weekend visits became intrusive, and Al's history with his dad exacerbated the situation. Al had, however, made a promise to his mother on her deathbed that he would take care of his father. Al would not break his promise, and I would not ask him to.

When the time came, we knew what we had to do. His dad moved in with us. Under the best of circumstances, caring for a parent poses difficulties. We didn't have the best of circumstances, but we did our best to fulfill Al's promise to his mother and keep his father safe, comfortable, and as happy as he ever allowed.

He lived with us for fifteen years until his death in February, 2010.

I felt a tap on my shoulder. I opened my weary eyes to see the airline attendant leaning over me.

"Is that your husband in the restroom?" she asked.

I looked to my left, saw the empty seat, and replied, "Yes."

She told me she had knocked on the bathroom door and hadn't gotten an answer.

I fought through my sleepy haze of a brain and remembered he had been gone a long time and I had thought he must have been having trouble negotiating the small room. How long had I been sleeping?

"He's not feeling well," I explained.

She asked if I would check on him. We walked to the front of the airplane to the restroom near the galley and cockpit door. She reached to the top of the door, flipped a lever or switch that only airline personnel would know, and the door swung open towards her to give me a little privacy.

He fell asleep, I thought. *He could sleep very soundly when he's this tired.*

I spoke his name . . . nothing. I spoke it again a little louder.

I lightly slapped his cheek, then a little harder.

He felt cold.

"He's not responding," I heard myself say.

When Al spoke, he said, "I think we should buy it." The "it" was a beautiful piece of property in the White Mountains of New Hampshire, in Bethlehem at the base of Twin Mountains with a river running along the back edge and the New Hampshire State Forest on the other side of the river. The owner had a small ramshackle trailer nestled up to a shed to create added living space, nothing we cared to keep, but we could see potential for saving the shed. Already clear of trees, the site would allow room for a decent-sized camp without much work, and enough trees remained to prevent too much exposure. The lot had running water and electricity. The outhouse would have to go, however.

We learned that the owner, from Florida, used the property as a hunting camp for himself and friends. Leaving piles of discarded appliances, tires, and trash in the woods behind the shed, they had clearly abused the land. It would take some time to clean up, but we thought the property ideal for our purpose.

On long holiday weekends, we had fallen into a routine of taking off on the motorcycles with our friends Jackie and Jerry. We headed up to the White Mountains and rode the Kancamagus Highway or up into Pittsburg to spot moose. We stayed in motels and ate out. It became expensive over time, so we discussed the idea of splitting the cost of a piece of land, possibly building a small camp or putting a trailer on the site.

As discussions became more serious, I started having doubts about whether the idea had merit. Not knowing if anyone else had the same apprehension, I questioned the notion. I know Al didn't—he wanted to own a camp all his life, and he spoke about it frequently. I had two concerns: should we buy property with friends and would we feel compelled to go to the camp every time we went on vacation, thus preventing us from traveling to other places?

The owner had the parcel on the market for quite some time. He owed back taxes, and we learned that he had grown tired of trying to maintain the camp from Florida. We also discovered that his parents sold him the lot for much less than what he asked for it. As the four of us considered whether to make an offer, Al said, "Let's offer him half."

The three of us laughed until we realized he meant it. Al started rambling off the costs of hauling away the trash, trailer, and tires. We began to see his point and decided, "What do we have to lose?" The Realtor relayed our offer, and after a little negotiation, the seller accepted our bid. The four of us bought a used two-bedroom camper and started cleaning up the property. In full disclosure, Jackie and Jerry did most of the work. Al and I worked six, sometimes seven days a week, making it difficult to find time to make the three-hour trip.

Nevertheless, we four spent many memorable days and nights in the White Mountains. A core group of friends and family often joined us. I call them our camp cohort, and we ate, drank, and laughed excessively. Mention Jiffy Pop to any one of them, and an instant smile will appear as we remember Al's kernel-popping dance around the fire pit. The video played well on social media. Or play the Minions ringtone on your cell phone and watch Jackie and Al break into uncontrollable, tear-producing laughter, no matter how many times you play it. And something we learned the hard way: never leave Al in charge of the birthday cake, especially if it's raining … "You had one job to do, Al!"

While popping Jiffy Pop, Al dances the Jiffy Pop dance around the campfire.

Jackie, Jerry, Al, and I hosted a wedding for our dear friends Kristy and Scotty on August 19, 2017. Kristy is Jackie's stepdaughter, and Al and I had known her since she was twelve years old. We all fell in love with Scotty the first time Kristy brought him to camp, so it seemed only fitting that they get married surrounded by family and friends there in the White Mountains.

In preparation for the big day, we doled out duties for everyone to perform. Al and I took the bar, a job for which we knew ourselves overqualified. We bought purple plastic cups, purple napkins, and purple straws to honor Kristy's favorite color, her wedding color. Comforted by the thought that, if it didn't get consumed at the wedding it would not go to waste, we bought an extensive assortment of liquor, beer, and mixes.

Al and I also wanted to do something special to remember the day, so I created a t-shirt graphic using the design from the wedding invitation and made shirts using the heat press we owned at our store. I pressed the white image on purple shirts

timed photo by Al Noyes

Most holiday weekends, the camp cohort gathers at the White Mountains of New Hampshire. They include, from left, the dog Shorty, Laura, Gary, Chris, Jerry, Jackie, the late Al, and Kristy.

of all sizes, a count of 125 of them, and we gave them to every guest at the wedding.

At the lower end of our property, a large tent fit nicely to house round tables covered with purple tablecloths. The live band with Kristy's brother as drummer, set up by the shed next to the bar. The ceremony took place in front of a small rock garden not far from our fire pits newly painted white with purple splashes. On the upper side of the property next to our camper, we set up the honeymoon suite—Kristy and Scotty's tent. The caterer smoked ribs, chicken, and brisket between the band set-up and the camper. We smelled cooking progress all day and felt nothing short of ravenous by the time we ate.

Not long before the ceremony, Kristy and Scotty presented Al with a floral head wreath to recognize him as honorary, behind-the-scenes flower girl. Scotty had offered him the position a few months earlier as we sat around the campfire, and Al ceremoniously accepted.

A perfect culmination of everyone working together and one of the most memorable weekends at camp, the wedding went off without a hitch.

Al rocks his floral wreath as unofficial flower girl at Kristy and Scotty's wedding in the White Mountains.

Everyone needs a happy place, a place where problems and worries vanish if only for a short time— place to sit by the campfire and listen to the rush of the river after a rainstorm or watch hummingbirds hover, sopping up their sweet nectar. Al and I had four such places numbered in order of importance and time frame. Camp was our third happy place. Although we could use it only on long holiday weekends, we talked about how we would spend much more time there once we retired.

HAPPY PLACE

So here I sit alone and tired, where we called Happy Place.
The hummingbirds you once admired flash by at a great pace.

The sun sets quickly on this day, and memories I chase.
Each day gets harder to display a smile upon my face.

They say in time I'll be okay, and grief I will embrace,
that God will help to show the way. I fear that's not the case.

Life moves on, in spite of things I can't help holding back,
for life means nothing without you—a purpose it does lack.

I work the store from day to day—business as usual.
My words are rote, no grief displayed. So many, then, I fool.

But as I sit here in this place, I know but one thing true.
The only thing I cannot face is my life without you.

  I met Jackie and Jerry at camp on Labor Day weekend, 2018. Al had been gone for about seven months, and I really had to push myself to make the trip up. As our large cooler sat on the tailgate of my truck, I filled it with food so I wouldn't have to lift it into the truck bed. I brought enough food so I wouldn't have to go shopping during my trip up north.

  I got there late in the afternoon. The rest of the camp cohort arrived at various times that day and the next. Once Gary showed up, I asked him for help taking the cooler out of the truck and placing it on the deck next to the shed. I had plenty of ice in my fifty-five quart Canyon Cooler, a pricey but well-made item we sold in our store. Stocked with food, it weighed perhaps sixty or seventy pounds.

  When I woke the next morning and went outside, I noticed the cooler missing. I asked Jerry and Jackie if they had moved it, and they said they hadn't. We searched the immediate area and came up empty. As unlikely as it seemed, I began to think someone had stolen it. Things like that just don't happen near our camp, but people who stay in nearby motels often get to the river along the path managed by the Town of Carroll water department at the edge of our property. Someone heading that way might find the cooler tempting.

We didn't want to believe that, and because of its weight, I reasoned it would take two people to haul it away. Maybe kids figured it had beer inside?

Jerry refused to believe any of it.

Jackie and I went shopping in nearby Littleton to replace some of the food. When we pulled into camp about two hours later, the cooler sat on the deck where I left it the night before. Jackie assured me I wasn't going crazy and corroborated it wasn't there when we left for the store.

Jerry came out of the trailer and explained.

The Case of the Missing Cooler, *one of Chris's children's books in the Big Al series published by Haley's, takes its plot from a bear's actual theft of a cooler.*

Unconvinced that someone stole the cooler, he searched the area and found drag marks in the lawn beside the shed. He followed the drag marks through broken limbs and mud into the woods, and about a hundred yards out, he spotted my cooler—unopened. He dragged the cooler back to camp, not an easy task. On inspection, he found bite marks and scratches undoubtedly made by a very large bear that must have found himself—or herself—extremely frustrated when unable to obtain the contents.

The thought occurred to me that the bear most probably skulked the proximity as Jerry retrieved the food, an unsettling prospect in itself.

I found myself fascinated by the amount of strength and fortitude required of the bear to accomplish its theft. I almost felt sorry that his or her efforts went unrewarded.

As for the food, the only casualty was one broken egg out of a dozen. After retelling the account to the rest of the crew when they came into camp for the day, I decided to write it as a children's story. I spent the next few hours creating a tale loosely based on events of the day, published as *The Case of the Missing Cooler*.

Not responding.

I suddenly found myself in the galley. Edging past me and forcing me to back up into the small service area, a young blonde woman—whom I believed to be a passenger waiting to use the restroom—squeezed between the open bathroom door and the first-class coat closet. She entered the tiny bathroom, and I watched as she placed her fingers on Al's throat to look for a pulse. She was very deliberate in her movements, making it obvious that she had some medical or training via First Responder Training. The flight attendant then opened the door fully in order to get to the cockpit telephone. I don't recall being able to hear what she said, which seems unlikely, because I stood only two feet away.

I began to feel ethereal as if constructed of vapors, not of this world but watching as the world unfolded before my eyes. What seemed like minutes must have passed in seconds as time became obsolete. I watched as the woman performed CPR on my husband. The only words I remember her saying? "I don't have a pulse" and "We have to get him out of here."

Two attendants, one on each side of the snack cart, had been serving drinks and snacks when it all began. They asked me to move in front of the cockpit door so they could put the cart back into the galley. Four of us then stood in the small space, making it impossible to secure the cart into its designated safe storage location. They asked me to hold on to the cart to keep it in place.

My hands began to shake.

Removing Al from the restroom required an arduous process excruciating to watch. The blonde woman, whose name I never learned and for whom I hold a great deal of gratitude and respect, enlisted help from some men seated in first class. They managed to get him out and lay him in the aisle on his back, head towards the cockpit, feet towards the tail. Expending an enormous amount of energy into every thrust of the chest, the blonde woman continued to perform CPR.

By then, every stranger on the plane was watching my husband die.

Because the forecast called for rain and wind the entire travel day, we trailered our motorcycles to Gettysburg. That July, we headed to Gettysburg Bike Week during one of the first years of the event. Organizers expected ten thousand bikers to attend.

Our decision to trailer the bikes and not ride four hundred miles turned out to be the right move, as the nasty weather proved relentless. Jackie, Jerry, Al, and I booked two rooms in an inexpensive motel between the town center and fairgrounds. Rain cleared by the next morning, and we had hot and sticky weather for the rest of week.

We mounted the motorcycles and, drinking in the history of our surroundings, toured the battlefields and stopped to read markers along the way, circled the rotary where President Lincoln gave the "Gettysburg Address," and rode the Cashtown Road to Cashtown Inn. Each day presented a new insight into history and a new adventure.

In more-than-ninety-degree heat, we journeyed single file down Emmitsburg Road, Jerry in the lead followed by Jackie, me, then Al. Shortly after we passed the infamous peach orchard, Jackie pulled to the side of the road. Al and I pulled in behind her, and once Jerry noticed, he turned around and joined us.

Jackie looked shaken. As we passed the peach orchard, she felt an extreme chill and the hair on her arms stood up, she explained. Al articulated the same thing. History tells us that fierce fighting and many casualties took place on July 2, 1863, in the peach orchard and immediate areas as well as in the entire battle. Many believe that the souls of some soldiers remain behind, unable to rest in peace.

I didn't feel anything unusual on that hot July day, but I have no doubt Jackie and Al did. Gettysburg exudes a kind of weightiness, a sensation of becoming one with sacred ground as if occupying every inch of air with no superfluous space on the lush green battlefields. Some people hear screams of soldiers and sounds of war as their battle continues, and others see apparitions of somnolent and disillusioned men.

That night, The Pike, the restaurant next to our motel, hosted a pig roast. We walked over early so we could grab seats on the outside deck before they filled up. At only four o'clock, the DJ worked on the deck as he set up his equipment for the evening.

Hot and hungry, we ordered a round of beer and appetizers to hold us over before dinner. The place filled up quickly with bikers, and soon the overflow reached into the parking lot with thousands of motorcycles. We parked our bikes safely in the trailer and knowing we would not ride that night . . . "Another round of drinks." The Pike prepared well for the event with plenty of food, drink, and entertainment, although most of us made our own entertainment.

With intoxicating beverages at The Pike restaurant in Gettysburg, Jackie, Chris, and Al, from left, prepare for his prize-winning feat.

At some point early in the evening, the DJ started music and tossed out the occasional question and trivia. Our table won the "traveled-the-farthest-to-get-here" award, though it did not come without protest. Some riders contended that we had trailered our bikes, not ridden them there, therefore disqualifying us. We acquiesced and abstained from taking our prize.

It came up on nine o'clock when the DJ started picking out contestants for his "sobriety check." We could tell he had paid attention to the crowd, as he picked out three of the most intoxicated men in the bunch. But he wanted one more. He looked directly at Al, pointed, and said, "You've been here for five hours drinking beer and you haven't gone to the bathroom. I want you!"

Al grudgingly joined the three others in line. They started with the nose-touching test, arms straight out to their sides, eyes closed, touching the tip of their noses with their index fingers. The observing crowd became the judges, and after each test we would applaud when the DJ pointed to the person who we decided had done best. They each received lukewarm results with two more tests before the finale. The second test had them stand on one leg while keeping balance. However fun to watch, each contender got the same lackluster result.

The last test challenged each participant to walk the line. The DJ stuck a ten-foot line of tape on the deck. He instructed each person to walk on the line, heel-to-toe for the full ten feet, then turn around and walk heel-to-toe back without faltering.

The first competitor wobbled his way to the end of the tape, turned, and walked back to finish upright. The second lost his balance partway on the first stretch and landed in the lap of a stranger at a nearby table. The steady third did a little better than the first. Then came Al's turn, and he knew he needed to stand out from the others, so he turned around and walked the line backwards heel-to-toe both ways, never wavering.

The intoxicated judges went wild, clearly pronouncing Al the winner. He won two sixteen-ounce Budweiser glasses that I still have in my cabinet today.

At the end of the contest, Al went to the bathroom.

A man appeared in the galley with me and was soon on the floor, opening a black case. He clearly wasn't one of the airline employees, so he must have been a passenger—a doctor, I assumed. He removed items from the case in the dark galley, and I thought he needed some light. "He could do this quicker if he had more light," I thought.

I looked above me and saw dozens of buttons and switches, but I didn't touch any of them. I kept thinking, "If this man could just have more light, everything would be all right."

I tried to explain to the flight attendant, but my words emerged almost silent as if someone had turned the volume down on my vocal cords. I asked her three times if one of the switches would provide light before she finally heard me, my volume still choked.

She flipped one of the switches to illuminate the galley, and I felt a sense of relief. "Everything will be all right now," I thought.

The man retrieved two paddles from his case.

I knew what would happen next.

We imagined Alaska as our dream vacation, the top of the bucket list. We originally planned our honeymoon to take us there but decided in favor of practicality and instead purchased a home. *We would have plenty of time to make the trip,* we thought. Before we knew it, almost twenty-five years went by. As our wedding anniversary approached, Vern and Mary made plans to go to Alaska and invited us to join them. What better way to celebrate?

But I blew it.

When I think back to that decision, as I often do, it reminds me of a ladder buckled, lying on the ground. "We can't afford it," I said and rattled on, listing all the reasons that mean so little now, "Maybe in a few years, but we can't afford it right now."

A few years passed, and I found myself on an airplane—surrounded by strangers—experiencing the worst day of my life.

Regret.

I will never go to Alaska.

I knew it had been taking him an unusually long time in the restroom. I wrestled with the thought, *Should I go check on him, see if everything is alright?* He was a large man in a tiny space, and my tired brain hurtled multiple possible scenarios at me, none of them pleasant. But I didn't want to embarrass him. I decided I would give him the time he needed. So I waited and closed my eyes.

Next thing I knew, a stranger asked me to check on my husband.

A double tap of guilt and regret, I am ashamed to admit.

"Clear," he said.

Everyone drew back as the paddles on either side of Al's chest sent a jolt through him.

We waited.

Another "Clear," another jolt.

For the first time since I felt that tap of guilt, the words, "What happens if . . . ?" crept into my head and "What if I had . . . ?"

It felt surreal. I couldn't fully process the contents of my own thoughts, fragments of a broken mirror that didn't fit together properly as they floated in the mist of my consciousness.

"Clear."

DISTANCE

The limbs blow cold with sleet and snow—a floor of white they have to show—
but in the distance far away the golden glow of the sun's ray.

The sting of heartache grabs my soul, a keen reminder of life's new hole.
But in the distance in the rafters breaks through tears the sound of laughter.

The humdrum days, the lonely nights at two AM in soft low light—
but in the distance where night is day, you stand and wait for me someday.

What plan could be this painful place? What point? I cannot see,
for in the distance, life awaits— that's where I want to be!

I know my time is not yet here. I have some things to do.
But every day is hard to bear while distance clings to you.

I'll do my part, for what it's worth, but this I must confess.
Without you with me on this earth, the distance scares me less.

Benches shook under the crowd of sixty thousand. Snow piling up on us as we sat in the bleachers flew once again as we jumped to our feet.

That's what playoff football looked like in New England on January 19, 2002. We played the Oakland Raiders, and the Patriots had trailed them for the entire game. In the waning moments of the fourth quarter, we were down by three points. Heavy snowfall had been a factor for both teams and the fans. The Portuguese moonshine we shared before the game lost its warming effect, so we huddled together on the cold metal benches of Foxboro Stadium.

The Patriots moved the ball almost to field goal range. Any true football fan knows what happened next: Charles Woodson of the Oakland Raiders sacked Tom Brady of the Patriots. As Brady went down, the ball came loose, and the Raiders recovered it. After review, officials determined that, even though it looked like Tom tucked the ball back into his body, he had been in the process of throwing it, so the action became an incomplete pass. No loss of yardage, no loss of possession in a situation later dubbed "The Tuck Rule" that made referee Walt Coleman an instant household name in New England.

When we saw the ball pop out of Brady's hand and recovered by Oakland, we were crushed. Our disappointment almost unbearable, the lowest of playoff lows, the stadium went almost silent . . . until Walt Coleman made his announcement.

We went from silent to full blown crazy in the time it took the Sahara roller coaster to go from zero to forty-five miles per hour. We literally never touched those benches again with everyone on their feet to watch Adam Vinatieri kick the field goal to tie up the score and go on to win the game in overtime during the last game in Foxboro Stadium.

The Patriots went on to win their first Super Bowl. The new stadium and the new Patriots era would arrive the following season.

We obtained our Patriots season tickets a couple years prior to that game, and I still hold on to them. As I write during twenty years as a season ticket holder, eighteen of them with Al, the Patriots have won six Super Bowl championships. Al lived to see five of them.

I knew. It would take nothing short of a miracle for Al to open his comforting blue eyes and tell me everything was going to be all right. I don't know how long I had been standing there shaking from my core, but I had nowhere to go, nowhere to hide, and no one to lean on.

They (and it was "they," strangers trying to save him) continued to perform CPR, first the woman, then the man, back and forth like a game of tag, the paddles apparently no longer a reasonable option.

I told myself that I couldn't give up hope, couldn't give in to my fears. Those people had not.

The flight attendant, the woman who had originally retrieved me from my seat, had been on the telephone, presumably speaking with the pilot. She leaned over to me and told me the plane would land soon. They would continue to work on Al, she told me. Therefore, we should stay put, stand right in place for the landing.

She asked me once again to hold the snack cart in place. I stood on the far side of the cart in the dark corner of the galley as she relayed her plan to do a countdown to touchdown so we could prepare. With the phone to her ear, she began counting backwards: twenty... nineteen... eighteen...

If ever there were heaven on earth, for us, Libby Camps exemplified it... our fourth happy place. Nestled in the northern Maine woods in the topo grid known as T8/R9, that remote and seemingly untouched region houses a family-owned sporting camp.

Libby family camps had previously hosted such guests as Teddy Roosevelt and Jack Dempsey. Matt and Ellen Libby of the fourth generation would soon host us.

Al stayed at Libby Camps multiple times, and he eagerly wanted me to experience it. Not much of a fisherman and certainly not a hunter by then, I didn't know what to expect. I suppose Al wanted to see if I would enjoy such a lifestyle. We had been dating for less than a year. Since the season hadn't yet opened, there would be no hunting on our trip. Fishing provided the principal motivation for most of their guests.

Using spruce and fir logs, the Libbys hand-built cabins each with a wood stove and kerosene lamps. Indoor plumbing would come later, and until then, the family provided a well-kept outbuilding with facilities and showers. Each cabin varied in size and layout: some could fit entire families with others meant for two. Every cabin faced Millinocket Lake, not the Millinocket Lake south of Baxter State Park but the other Millinocket Lake between Baxter

Phil Johnson, left, and Al show off their catch.

and Aroostook counties. I've never understood why Maine has two lakes with the same name.

Each cabin has a picture window overlooking a front porch and, just beyond, the pristine lake. Guests gather for companionship and meals in the main lodge, also hand-built with a large full-length porch overlooking the lake and spectacular sunsets.

Although best known for trout and landlocked salmon fishing, the camp's food became the highlight of my stay. Ellen prepared everything from scratch every day. With no electricity, she kept food cold with ice chopped, stacked, and stored underground in a large shed. The Libbys used the gas generator on site only for emergencies or special occasions. The large butcher block table in the kitchen constantly held bowls of rising bread dough along with a pleasant aroma of whatever Ellen prepared. From a boat on the lake if the wind shifted just right, the smell made us hungry.

Except for breakfast with a choice of eggs, pancakes, or whatever specialty Ellen prepared, the Libbys served food family style. For early risers who went fishing before breakfast, Ellen cooked up what they caught and served it with eggs. Anglers shared their success, so other guests could have fish pretty much any day.

When we could afford it, we chose the easiest, fastest and most exciting way to get to Libby Camps: by float plane. Matt had his pilot's license and flew people in from Bangor, where we left our vehicle after the four-hour drive from Massachusetts. For a truly memorable adventure, he could also fly us out to the remotest of areas. Even the most novice of fishermen like me would usually have success on Millinocket Lake, but on one of our stays, neither one of us had much luck catching fish on the lake or nearby rivers, so Matt told us to pack up our rods and tackle boxes and follow him.

*Al basks in his element on the lake at
Libby Camps in the woods of northern Maine.*

We hopped into the Cessna and soared over a legion of lakes, rivers, ponds, and streams until he settled us down on one: a small body of water in the middle of nowhere with a motorboat onshore. He handed us two bag lunches and told us he'd be back at four.

And he was gone.

As we watched the plane skip on the water and then rise into the air, we began to realize our situation. We had no idea where we were and had no way to contact anyone. Only Matt knew we were there, deep in the heart of wilderness. We felt like the last two people on earth—thrilled yet intimidated, exhilarated yet vulnerable. In other words, perfect.

We spent the day with a freedom we had never before experienced, unbound from obligations, anxiety, or accountability—just the two of us on a boat in a lake. Somewhere.

We still didn't catch any fish.

On a separate trip to Libby Camps, we drove our pre-owned bright red Ford Festiva packed to the gills with our clothes and fishing equipment. The spectacle of the jam-packed little car with its challenged suspension resembled the Flintstones mobile from the 1960s cartoon series.

Other than flying in on a float plane, access to Libby Camps involved navigating to the privately owned logging roads of the Great Northern Paper Company. Built for logging truck use and not for public traffic, the crude, unpaved narrow passages suffered from harsh Maine winters. It seemed that a pothole had to equal the size of a small car before anyone deemed it worthy of repair.

The public can use the roads by paying a fee to the paper company with agreement the logging trucks have the right of way. As we traveled in our weighed-down Festiva, it's no wonder we seemed somewhat preposterous travelers as we paid our toll.

While driving the oddly named Golden Road we encountered a few big rigs hauling full loads of logs. We dutifully pulled over as close to the side of the road as possible as the trucks screamed toward us. Once, we pulled over for Al to check the map to make sure of our course.

As Al confirmed our route, a car pulled in behind us, thus adding to quite a bit more traffic on the road than we anticipated.

Apparently imagining us in distress, an enforcement officer approached our little red box of a car.

Maybe he thought we had gotten stuck in a pothole.

We assured him we were fine.

He advised us not to stop again and told us it wasn't safe to do so, especially considering our vehicle and its load.

We thanked him for checking on us and got on our way circumnavigating the cavities in the earth.

As we arrived at Libby Camps, Matt happened to be working near the driveway entrance and spotted us in the absurd little vehicle. He burst into laughter at the sight. After initial hugs and hellos, Al felt the need to explain the reasoning for our transportation.

On his way to work not long before as he drove his pickup truck through West Boylston, another pickup truck hit his. Al got some bumps and bruises, and the insurance company deemed his truck totaled. The payout for the truck afforded us just enough money to buy the lowly Ford Festiva.

A few days after we arrived, the sun rose to a clear blue sky and warmed the day to perfection. Al and I decided to take our fly rods and venture out to a nearby river to a place called Devil's Elbow far enough away from camp that we had to drive.

Ellen packed us each a bag lunch and, directions in hand, we set out to catch some fish. We found a spot off the road to pull our car safely out of danger from the trucks. We gathered our waders, rods, nets, tackle, and small cooler and proceeded down a steep wooded embankment about thirty feet down to the water. In a treeless riverside opening, we donned our waders and stored the gear.

We spent the next four hours in the crystal-clear water just around the bend of a sharp elbow turn in the river. Water rushed around us under a cerulean blue sky. We basked in a shower of sunlight. Most of the fish escaped us, but we reeled in a few and scooped them into the nets that attached to the back of our waders before we released them back into the pristine stream.

At about two o'clock, we decided to return to the riverbank and eat our lunch. We worked our way back to shore over to our stash of goods and began to take off our wet neoprene waders. Just then, our supremely relaxing and perfect day took a turn.

Removing wet waders is like peeling a layer of skin and happens incrementally and slowly. Just as we began, we noticed a dark little flash above our heads. Agreeing it must have been a bird, we got back to the task at hand.

Seconds later we saw a dark figure swooping down toward us. It caused both of us to duck as we feared it might hit us in the head. The thing sped back up into the tree-lined sky and we lost sight of it.

I looked at Al and saw the confusion that I felt in his eyes. A bat had just lunged at us in the middle of a beautiful sunlit day. It could not be good.

We hurriedly but unsuccessfully tried to extricate our waders before the bat returned. The little creature reappeared and made a series of dives directly at us, leaving little time between attempts for us to get free of our encumbering wetsuits.

We made a plan for me to use the fishing net attached to the neck of my waders to keep the bat at bay while Al got himself free. On its next approach, I stood between it and Al as I stretched the net's elastic cord out as far as I could manage in order to scare the flying mammal away by swiping at it. As it got close to me, the bat stretched out its wings, its claws reaching out in front, and its little beady black eyes seemed to look directly into mine.

As the bat swooshed by about three feet away from me, I swung and narrowly missed it with the fishing net's wooden rim. The action must have looked like a child throwing a ball, my movement restricted by the net's elastic cord prohibiting a full swing.

The bat retreated once more but didn't waste much time before it tried again. With Al finally free of his waders and his boots back on his feet, the animal attacked again.

"This time," I said to Al, "I'm going to try to catch it in the net."

Both of us had our nets at the ready with Al's detached from his waders. Our angry, usually nocturnal menace decided to head in my direction again. It plunged quickly and intently as I readied myself.

Timing as best I could, I swung the net like a tennis racket and intended to trap it in the mesh but instead hit it with the rim, thus driving it to the ground. With a speed I had never seen him move, Al jumped on the bat and ground it into the earth, twisting his boot-clad foot with enormous pressure—so much that when he lifted his foot from the ground we could almost not determine the bat from the dirt.

The experience rattled us. Having no further interest in staying in the area, I removed my waders, and we gathered up our belongings to head back up the embankment to the car. We had passed a camping spot on the way to the aptly named Devil's Elbow and remembered it had a picnic table and fire pit. Apparently, the paper company allowed tent camping for a fee in certain areas.

We decided to head there to eat our lunch. We parked the car off the road and walked into the camping area. Seated at the picnic table across from one another, we opened our bags each containing—thanks to Ellen—a roast beef sandwich on fresh-baked bread, potato chips, bottled water, and a homemade cookie.

I found myself swatting at a wasp as it circled my lunch bag. Not thinking much of it, I continued to unpack the food. I looked over at Al, and he, too, swatted at a wasp. Then there was another one—and another—and another. Soon a hoard of wasps surrounded us as we each frantically waved our arms to shoosh them away.

We looked under the tabletop and found a nest as big as a basketball. We quickly headed back to the car which would serve by default as our dining room. Feeling secure that the wasps had not followed us, we opened the windows on that beautiful warm day. At last, we commenced eating our meal.

It tasted delicious. Happy to be rid of the situation, we attempted to shrug off the scary and unfortunate events of the day with nervous laughter.

About to take another bite of my sandwich, I got a glimpse of movement beside me outside the passenger window. I turned my head and saw a bright green, almost neon-color, flying insect about three inches long hovering at eye level. Its wings beat as quickly as a hummingbird's, but it didn't move an inch.

Neither one of us could identify the flying insect, and to this day, I could not.

I swiftly rolled up my window as Al turned the key to start the car. We pulled out to the logging road and headed back toward Libby Camps. The glowing green bug stayed with us, matched our speed, and remained at eye level for close to a mile.

Once sure we had rid ourselves of the unknown creature, Al stopped the car in the middle of the road. With windows closed and the car running, we finished our lunch. We returned to camp and related the day's events to Matt, Ellen, and a few guests in the lodge.

All of us agreed that the bat must have been rabid or it would not have been out during the middle of a sunny day. As for the large green insect, nobody had ever seen anything like it. It remains a mystery.

We told our Hitchcockian story many times over the years, and each time I see it vividly in my memory. As alarming as our encounter with the bat, we always considered Devil's Elbow one of the most beautiful places we ever visited.

Once we were on the ground, things seemed to happen very quickly. The air controllers must have cleared the tarmac to give us priority, because we quickly reached the gate. The jetway door opened in only a matter of a minute or two.

EMTs stood at the door. The two people who had performed CPR backed away to allow the EMTs to take over. Four of them lifted Al and swiftly moved him to the jetway where a gurney waited, but they didn't put him on it. They laid him down on the gangway, stuck an IV in his arm, and placed a large square machine, about the size of a small generator, on his chest. On each side of the machine, they put Al's hands through a carrying grip so he seemed to cradle the object to his body. Once the EMTs turned on the machine, a large cylinder with a black padded cover repeatedly dropped down on Al's chest like a relentless rhythmic boxer during a match.

Thump, thump, thump . . .

And then I saw the drill.

In November of 1987, shortly after our first date and the night before Thanksgiving, Al said he would stop by to see me at my Dad's house to say goodbye because he expected to leave on a hunting trip early the next day. My mother and two sisters came by to help peel vegetables and make pies for our feast at Dad's the next day. Despite the divorce, we still gathered as a family for holidays. I had ill-advisedly mentioned to my mother and sisters beforehand that Al planned to come by, thus giving them plenty of time to plan their humiliation of me. When Al arrived, he barely had time to scan the room before they plopped him into a chair in the middle of the kitchen. They sang to him a song they created from the little bit of information they cleverly extracted from me.

I was mortified but couldn't help falling into side-splitting laughter as I curled up on the floor leaning against the cabinets. Al handled it surprisingly well, laughing all the while. But it wasn't his usual hearty, deep-chested laugh. It sounded more like a cheerful "Should-I-run-now?" laugh. Thank goodness, he didn't.

That would not be the last time my family made up songs and sang to Al. On at least two other occasions, they would feel the need to do so—once at our wedding shower in front of all our friends and family and another at a Christmas gathering with the theme being the twelve days of Christmas. That song included fishing rods, venison, and five Christmas ties.

Al had hunted since he was a teenager. He learned from a family friend because his father had no interest in the time-honored tradition. He learned to handle every weapon, whether a firearm or bow, with extreme care and respect. He also had enormous respect for the animals he hunted. He subscribed to the fair chase method and never shot anything he didn't plan to eat. On the other hand, I had little enthusiasm about the prospect of him going out and shooting a beautiful deer or bear.

Fortunately for me, he had never actually killed one, so I felt safe when I choked out a "Good luck" as he set off on his trip. Apparently, that was all he needed. When he came home, he had a cooler full of venison and a chest full of pride. I felt happy for him, but I still didn't want to eat that meat.

As years passed, I grew to feel much different about the heritage of hunting and the food it produced. Al explained the importance of maintaining the deer population and other species. I found out about fair chase and the ethical nature of following its rules. He showed me what happens when the population exceeds the food source, a horrible thing to think about and Nature's way of maintaining the population. Nature can be cruel.

I've since met many people who live off the land, whether through gardening, hunting, or both. Once we learned not to overcook the venison it became our favorite meat to eat. And it doesn't get more organic than that.

"What's the drill for?" I asked the person standing next to me.

When I didn't get a response, I looked up to see the man with the nice face, the pilot, also looking confused and concerned. I hadn't noticed when he came out of the cockpit.

Addressing the man holding it, I asked again, "What's the drill for?"

He told me that sometimes it would help revive the patient—blood flow or something like that. I couldn't grasp his meaning, because what I saw horrified me. He had begun to drill into Al's lower leg.

I remember thinking, *God help me. I hope he is dead.* I couldn't bear the thought that he might feel what was happening to him.

While all that transpired, somehow the airline employees managed to get our luggage out of the cargo hold and our carry-ons off the plane to set them in the jetway. They lifted Al onto the gurney, and we were off. By then, eight or ten people surrounded us. Each grabbed luggage and equipment, and one stuck by my side. With EMTs guiding the gurney, we raced on foot through the airport to the ambulance and emergency vehicle waiting outside, where they directed me to the front seat of the ambulance.

I suddenly realized I had to contact my brother to let him know what was going on. I asked them what hospital we headed to, and they wrote the name down on a piece of paper: Moses H. Cone Memorial Hospital, Greensboro.

I took my cell phone out of airplane mode and dialed my brother's number.

I didn't know if he would answer and I didn't know if they were already in the air, since I hadn't thought to check the time.

He answered.

"Al collapsed on the plane," I choked out. "It doesn't look good. I don't think he's going to make it."

I didn't have definitive medical information, so I didn't want to tell him what I believed—that he was already gone.

There was a moment of silence on the other end of the phone. I hated that I had to blurt it out like that, but I didn't know how much time we had.

My brother and his wife had been about to board their plane when I called.

"Where are you?" he asked. "We'll be there as soon as we can," he said. I looked at the paper and told him we were headed to Moses H. Cone Memorial Hospital, Greensboro, Atlanta.

I would later realize that what I told him didn't make sense, but I surely wasn't thinking clearly.

Six months earlier, in June, we packed up Mary's SUV, and Mary, Vern, Al, and I headed off to Tennessee. Our niece, their daughter, recently had a baby girl, and Al and I hadn't met her, so off we went.

A beautiful baby with huge brown eyes and the longest eyelashes we had ever seen, she took to Al right away, flashing her smile and winning his heart instantly. We spent the next lazy day enjoying family. The second day, we took a ride through the Smoky Mountains, stopping now and then for shopping and eating. We even got treated to some wildlife on the way down the backside of the magnificent mountains

Al, Chris, Mary, and Vern, from left, take in the Smoky Mountains during a trip celebrating Al and Vern's sixtieth birthdays.

as we headed into Gatlinburg. Mary spotted a bear and her two cubs off in the woods. Both she and Al had their cameras out, snapping as many pictures as they could before the bears moved back into the hills. Al made one of the pictures into a canvas that hangs on our wall back home.

The four of us left the next morning for Kentucky.

Late in the afternoon, we stopped at Logan's Roadhouse restaurant somewhere between Lexington and Louisville. Even at that early dinner hour, the dining room was close to full. The host seated us at a table of four next to windows at the back of the restaurant, Mary and I closest to the outside view, Vern and Al in the aisle chairs. Our server, a young, thin blonde woman with a thick Kentucky accent, approached us with well-worn menus and an empty smile. She asked if we would like a drink before ordering our food. Al, Vern, and I ordered beer, and Mary ordered a mixed drink.

When our server returned to our table with her hands full, she had one of the long-neck beers nestled into her armpit. She bent at the waist, her half-covered bust prominently exposed at eye level to Al, and asked him, "Could you grab this, Honey?"

The look on Al's face was priceless, but he did as she asked and, carefully avoiding an inadvertent brush against her boob, retrieved the bottle. She placed the rest of the drinks on the table and sauntered away.

We couldn't hold it in. The four of us burst out with laughter a little too loud, perhaps, but well deserved. When the young waitress returned, she began telling us a story about her momma. She told us her momma liked to slam her beer down on the table, presumably provoking an eruption of froth, and then chug it before she lost any of the precious brew. But, as Momma had warned her daughter and her daughter relayed to us, "Now, Honey, don't you slam it if you ain't gonna chug it!"

Before taking our order, she went on for ten more minutes about her momma and also about her long day at work and how she couldn't wait to get out of there. The hilarity of her tale almost too much for us to hold in, it took every ounce of restraint we could muster not to erupt again. She held us hostage in a backwoods Kentucky drama, and the starring role went to her, whom we dubbed Eunice.

We quoted Eunice often during our Kentucky trip and beyond. We found a waitress in Louisville who could have been her alter ego (we dubbed her Urban Eunice) who could barely carry a tray or a conversation. If I wrote a sitcom about the two women, it would be called *Chug and Lug*. Because all four of us worked in restaurants at one time or another and knew the hard work it entailed and because of the amount of entertainment value they provided, we left each of them a hefty tip.

For the record, we found the people of Kentucky wonderful, generous, and gracious. We had just enough luck to run into two of the state's more colorful and callow citizens. And I don't mean any disrespect to women named Eunice: we took the name from one of the star's characters on the sixties and seventies *Carol Burnett Show*.

We had reservations in a hotel in Louisville, slated to be our home base as we celebrated Al and Vern's sixtieth birthdays by doing what we do best—drinking bourbon. The Kentucky Bourbon Trail held a spot on the bucket list and seemed the perfect way to commemorate sixty years times two. The Kentucky Bourbon Distillers Association recommends taking nine days for the tour. We had only three days, and we added some distilleries to the mix even though they didn't have a place on the official tour.

We would have to plan well. Time was of the essence.

We used the GPS to get us efficiently from one place to another. We planned each day according to regions and planned our meals suitably to eat fast and move on with snacks and water in the car between stops.

Each distillery had specific tour operating hours. If we could arrive at a distillery at nine o'clock in the morning and plan accordingly, we might be able to pull off seeing all the distilleries we wanted to see within three days.

We drove through some of the most picturesque and perfectly groomed landscape I ever saw, especially in Versailles with miles of manicured horse country, post-and-beam fences separating the fields, and horse barns bigger and more ornate than resorts back home. The drive became part of the experience as we saw that incredible countryside, one farm after another.

We averaged five distilleries a day, each with a tasting tour, a feat by itself with plenty of driving distance between some stops. As we headed to the last stop on the second day, I put the GPS coordinates into my smart phone, and off we went. After we traveled for more than half an hour Mary said, "This doesn't seem right. Weren't we supposed to go back the way we came? I don't recognize any of this."

I checked the GPS and found us on the right course but headed to the wrong place. The distillery had two separate tours, one at the distillery and the other at its bottling plant and warehouse. To qualify for the official tour we only needed to visit one of the two, so we chose the bottling plant and warehouse as closest and most convenient.

Instead of the warehouse address, I put the address for the distillery into the GPS, so it would take us an extra hour to get to our destination. If we didn't get there in time, we couldn't complete the tour. It would take too long to drive back to the distillery, and on top of that, we wouldn't have time to drive to all the stops we had scheduled for the third day.

Had I just blown it? Would we miss out on the coveted free t-shirt honoring completion of the Official Bourbon Trail? Already halfway to the wrong place, we decided to keep going. I checked the hours of operation and, if we hurried, we would arrive exactly at closing time.

As we pulled into the driveway, I jumped out of the moving car, and ran to the door. It opened.

As it turned out, we weren't the only late arrivals. A couple came in shortly after us, so distillery personnel decided to do one more tasting.

I felt relieved. I didn't want to be the cause of coming up short.

Another case of the silly things we fret about on an average day.

The discovery of our love for bourbon was not accidental. It was coerced one Sunday at family dinner. We sat around the dining room table after finishing our meal hours earlier when my brother poured Al a short glass of bourbon.

"I don't like bourbon," Al said.

"You'll like this one," Vern countered. "Just try it."

A pained look on his face, Al gagged on the first sip. The glass contained only a small amount, so Al politely finished it.

My brother went to refill, and Al repeated, "I really don't like bourbon."

"You really didn't like it?" Vern asked as he reached for another bottle. "Try this one."

He poured a different brand into Al's glass.

I could see what was happening, so I put down my beer and drank water for the rest of the night.

One by one, my brother tried different brands of bourbon and whiskey on Al. Each received the same response of distaste from Al until Vern got to a particular brand. Al took a sip, smiled, and said, "This is pretty good."

I don't know if Al was too inebriated to taste what he drank or if he really liked it. What I do know is that episode began our love affair with bourbon. Hard to believe, but true.

Family dinner was Mary's idea. At a funeral, we discussed that we saw each other as a family only on holidays or as the result of some tragic event. Holidays always felt busy and rushed while funerals and wakes felt somber and sad. So Mary suggested that we start a new tradition: family dinner at their house in Warren about thirty miles from our home in Orange on the first Sunday of every month. She would cook, and we only had to commit to showing up whenever possible. If we couldn't make it, we should just make sure to let her know so she could plan.

We all agreed, and a new tradition was born. With schedules as diverse and busy as ours, you would think it impossible to accomplish, but because we knew well in advance not to schedule anything else on those Sundays, it became easy.

My father particularly enjoyed the arrangement. He never missed a family dinner and often arrived first. Al and I sometimes missed due to a Patriots game or holiday weekend at camp, but we made all the others. Paula came whenever possible even though she then lived in Vermont, so she found it harder to schedule. When she committed to walking across the country, she found attendance even more challenging. Our nieces and nephews, some with their own children, also tried their best to attend. The plan gave us a wonderful opportunity to watch their kids grow up and spend time together. Some of Mary's family often stopped in after dinner, and sometimes we played games or, more often, simply sat and talked. Vern and Mary have since moved from their house in Warren, but they continue to host family dinner in the new home they purchased in our hometown. I will always cherish

Mary and Al laugh heartily as they always did on occasions that brought them together.

the memories created at their former address and continue to appreciate the memories we make at our Sunday gatherings.

After a very long fifteen-minute drive, we pulled into the emergency room entrance, and the EMTs immediately wheeled Al into the first room on the left. Someone brought our luggage in and set it in the hallway. Like another piece of luggage, I stood in the hall motionless, staring at the green curtain the medical people had pulled closed for privacy.

Only moments later, the doctor came out and spoke to me. "We're still trying, but it doesn't look good. We're going to keep trying," he said as he ducked back behind the curtain.

Ten minutes later, he came back out. "There was nothing we could do. He was gone before he got here. I'm very sorry."

And there it was, spoken out loud, which somehow made it more real. My husband, my best friend, my soulmate, my Love. Gone.

It was nine o'clock in the morning.

Someone led me into the room where, on a stainless-steel table, Al lay covered from his shoulders to his feet with a thin white sheet. A nurse asked if I wanted time alone with him. They would give me privacy, take all the time I needed, she said.

I spoke with him. I kissed him. I cursed him for leaving me. I sat in silence with him. But mostly, I cried.

The impact of my loss didn't fully hit right away. My awareness came in dribbles like an IV injecting just a little dose at a time. Maybe it was a built-in coping mechanism or maybe it was just shock. It's hard to say. What I do know is that the IV continues to drip, even today.

I had to call my sister Paula. She was in Hawaii, and I didn't know the time there. I dialed her number, and she answered. I told her what had happened. We cried.

She asked where I was, and I told her we were in a hospital in Atlanta.

As I told her, a nurse walked into the room to retrieve something. She turned to me and said, "Oh, Honey. You're not in Atlanta. You're in Greensboro, North Carolina. The airplane made an emergency landing."

I immediately began to panic. I told Paula I would call her back and hung up on her. Vern and Mary would be heading to Atlanta if I didn't reach them in time.

Thank goodness Vern answered his phone. I told him my mistake, that we were in Greensboro, not Atlanta. They had already changed their flight to go to Atlanta. They would have to go back to see what they could do.

I bet Al got a good laugh at my expense right about then. What the hell? Greensboro? Atlanta?

When I left the room, I didn't know it would be the last time I would see Al.

A woman sitting behind a desk in the emergency room suggested I go to the cafeteria. She walked me there, pointed out where I could get food and coffee, then returned to her post.

I bought a cup of coffee and sat facing the door, hoping to go unnoticed, wishing I could fade away in the furthest corner of the cafeteria. The events of the morning replayed over and over in my mind like a vinyl record with a stuck needle as I wondered if I could have saved him had I checked on him sooner instead of worrying about embarrassing him. Wishing I hadn't closed my eyes. Wishing we hadn't got on the plane.

I called Paula back after clearing up plans with Vern and Mary, who had to fly through Atlanta to get to Greensboro anyway, so they didn't have to change their flight again. It would be seven hours before they landed in North Carolina. Paula made plans to fly in from Hawaii, a fourteen-hour trip. She called our older sister, Pam, who lives in Mexico, to tell her the news. Pam called me while I was in the hospital cafeteria. I hadn't spoken to her since my father passed away.

I sipped my coffee. Although I hadn't given much thought to my next move, I assumed I would wait in the hospital cafeteria until Vern and Mary arrived. Sometime later, two women walked through the door, looked around the room, and then focused their eyes on me. They approached with faint smiles and introduced themselves as employees of Delta Airlines. They told me that they would help me with anything I needed.

They asked if they could call anyone, and I explained I had already been in touch with my family who made arrangements to meet me in Greensboro. Straightaway they took charge, obtained the flight information for my brother and sister-in-law, and made plans to pick them up at the airport as soon as they arrived. We retrieved our luggage from the security office where it had been stored. We headed to the Marriot Hotel, where they procured two rooms, one for me and one for Vern and Mary. Paula wouldn't arrive until the next morning. She would take the hotel shuttle when she got in and share the room with me.

I must have been at the hospital for several hours because once we reached my room overlooking the airport, the Delta Ladies, as I began to think of them, asked if they could take me downstairs to the dining room for lunch. I thanked them for their help, but feeling the need to be alone, I declined. They left me with a stack of food vouchers for later use. I was grateful they whisked me away from the cafeteria. I craved isolation.

I sometimes still find myself sitting, staring at the wall, my brain devoid of thoughts, seeing only pictures unfold as I did in that hotel room for many hours on the day it all transpired. After a time, though, I realized I needed to make some phone calls.

I began with Al's boss after finding the number in Al's cell phone. I never met him, although Al spoke of him as if he were an old friend. Al worked at Markem-Imaje Corporation for less than a year, I could hear the news hitting him with shock and complete surprise. The reaction would replay multiple times in the following hour.

I waited to call Skip because I knew that once I called him, news would spread fast. I wanted to make sure that my family and our closest friends didn't hear about it secondhand.

Skip worked for us. He wandered into the store only months after we opened, and as I always did, I immediately approached my new customer and asked, "Is there anything I can help you find?"

He said, no, he was just looking, adding that he didn't know that our store was there. He had recently moved to the area. He used to be a professional archer sponsored by Browning, and he worked at a big box sporting goods store but didn't like it very much.

He asked if we were hiring.

I explained how we had just recently opened and couldn't afford to hire anyone.

He went on to tell me his life story, as many people would do in the coming years. Being owner of a gun and bow shop somehow equates you to a drink slinger behind a bar (fittingly, when I closed the store, I took the retail counter home and turned it into a bar).

Skip told me how he grew up in Framingham and traveled to shoots. He said he held a lot of archery records in

Massachusetts and frequented a place called Forest Orchard Sports in Westboro.

Wondering how I could extricate myself from him to finish my paperwork, I nevertheless quietly listened to his story, until I heard the words "Forest Orchard Sports."

"Don and Connie's shop?" I asked.

He looked surprised, considering Westboro lies a bit more than an hour from Orange and our shop. He asked how I knew Don.

I told him that my husband helped in their store sometimes, and at the sportsmen's show in Worcester. When I told him my husband's name, I didn't expect his response.

"Not Big Al. Are you kidding?" he asked. "I got us thrown out of a strip club during his bachelor party!"

That was news to me, so I was compelled to listen to the rest of the story. Apparently, the club owner thought the guys had gotten a little too loud, and by that I mean Skip got too rambunctious, and asked them to leave. Al later told me the dancers were furious they got evicted, because they had been making a fortune off his group.

How was it that I had never met this man?

We eventually hired Skip for his archery and sales experience. If anything, he would keep our customers entertained.

He was crushed when I called him about Al. He had known Al for almost forty years.

And I was right about how the news would spread, although I was oblivious to just how rapidly.

Sitting in the quiet hotel room, I was numb—my mind, my body, and my soul. Once or twice I got up and looked out the window, but mostly I just sat watching pictures rush through my head as tears spilled down my face. I felt the heft of the day in my chest. I couldn't stop wondering why we never discussed canceling the trip, why it never occurred to us just to stay home, why I didn't check on him . . . an endless stream of weighty whys.

The Delta Ladies met Vern and Mary at the baggage claim and brought them straight to my room. I could see the stress of the day in their faces and unbearable sadness in their eyes. They looked like me—trampled. We cried, and then we talked. I told them everything. I had to get the images out of my head, and I hoped by talking about them they would go away, but they didn't. Talking about them just made them more real, but Vern and Mary needed to know. He was their family, too.

Al called Vern Little Brother, and Vern called Al Big Brother. They were born the same year only three months apart. No one can recall exactly when they created the nicknames but I know where they conceived them—on the back deck in the backyard of Vern and Mary's house in Warren, our second happy place, during what we called Family Dinner 2.0. Family Dinner 2.0 happened when the rest of the family went home and Vern, Mary, Paula (when available), Al, and I remained.

Al, left, and Vern—Big Brother and Little Brother— brew up some of their habitual spirited mischief in 2017.

In warmer months, we sat out under the canopy dressed in white lights, on the two-tiered deck overlooking the brick patio with a fire pit and pleasingly landscaped lawn. During Family Dinner 2.0, the bourbon, wine, and spirits freely flowed. With Clapton or another great artist playing in the background, Vern, Al, and I lit our cigars and completely and utterly relaxed.

One evening, after we had been imbibing for quite some time, Vern came out of the house with a stack of hats retrieved

Siblings Paula, Vern, and Chris sip spirits on Vern and Mary's deck about 2017.

from his closet . . . which overflowed with hats. He plunked one on each of our heads without saying a word. Some of the hats fit well and looked great, others not so much, but without question, we kept them on. About twenty minutes later, Vern called out "Switch," took off his hat, and traded with one of us. We followed his lead, and thus began the hat tradition.

group selfie by Al Noyes

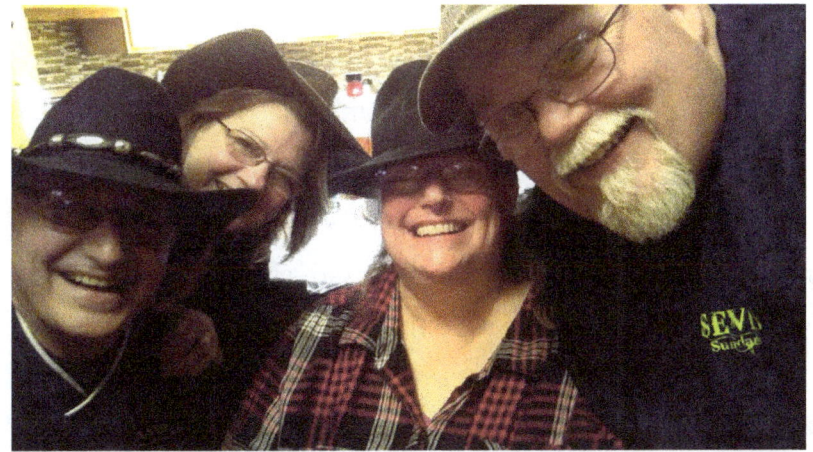

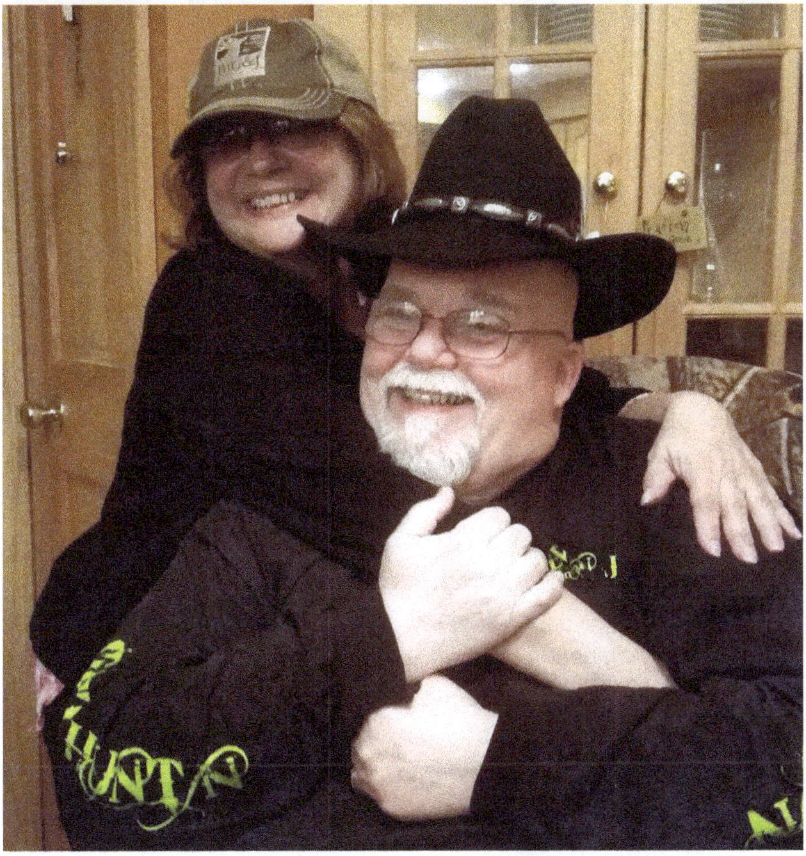

photo by Christine Noyes

Vern, Mary, Chris, and Al enjoy combined Hat Night/Mai Tai Night, top, and Mary and Al hug at Vern and Mary's after exchanging hats about 2016

Anyone could say "Switch." It was a silly little game, no reason behind it, no winner or loser, no strategy or stress, but it did make for some great photo opportunities.

I am staggered by the things I miss most, moments that trigger a memory whether happy or sad, situations that will never be quite the same, silly games we regarded as trivial. What I wouldn't give to have realized that when I made excuses not to take that trip to Alaska, spend money on an item that would have given us much joy, or simply closed the store for a day just to spend time together.

More regrets.

ANOTHER DAY WITHOUT YOUR SMILE

Another day without your smile. Your laugh I do not hear.
I lie in bed just for a while, pretend that you are near.

I make my bed and brush my teeth. My morning routine goes
when all the while my soul beneath knows emptiness that grows.

Sixteen months have passed me by. Each day runs into next.
On memories I must rely, but still my soul is vexed.

I write, each day, another page of how life used to be.
If truth be told, I try to gauge how much people should see.

The joy you shared while you were here I cherish every day.
So many things that I could share but will keep some at bay.

Not everything must now be told. Some secrets I will keep
until such time your hand I hold next to you as I sleep.

Word spread quickly at home. I began getting texts, emails, and a few phone calls. Some I responded to, others I didn't. There would be many people I should talk to. I just wasn't ready.

I may have been aware of the passage of time but I have no recollection of it. As I remember the events of the day, even today, it feels like it all happened in an abyss, a vacuum of time, encapsulated in a bubble where the minutes just circled around me, no beginning and no end.

Vern, Mary, and I went downstairs to the dining room. It was the first time I left the room. The sun had set.

We picked a table near the bar. Even though I hadn't eaten all day, I wasn't hungry. Nevertheless, I ordered something, and we sat picking at our food in near silence.

Once we went back upstairs, Vern and Mary brought their luggage next door to the room that the Delta Ladies reserved for them. They decided, however, they would stay with me that night in my room's other double bed. At some point, the worst day of my life ended with the three of us falling asleep in a hotel room in Greensboro, North Carolina, as exhaustion became my temporary savior from ruminations.

Paula went to Hawaii as part of her Happiness Walk. She co-founded a group called Gross National Happiness USA, an organization trying to change policy about the way our country measures its success and wellbeing. The organization's title plays on the words gross national product, the current way our government measures our success.

As part of her commitment to GNHUSA, Paula walked across the country meeting and interviewing individuals to try to find out what they consider most important in their lives. From the website:

> GNHUSA comprises part of a growing global happiness movement that emphasizes happiness and wellbeing at the center of our decision-making and policy discussions.

She had already walked the entire east, south, and west coasts of the continental US and had gone to Hawaii to walk while taking advantage of nice January weather. Not surprisingly, her interviews reveal that family ranks among top responses of people she asks, "What matters most in life?"

Fatefully, she found herself on her way to Greensboro, North Carolina, to join her grieving family.

When Paula resumed her walk, she finished up with Hawaii and headed back to Yakima, Washington, where she had previously stopped before winter kicked in. Then she headed southeast and, on her way through Idaho, deposited some of Al's ashes into the beautiful Snake River, one of our bucket list places that went unvisited.

My brother, sister, and sister-in-law remained by my side for as long as I needed them. I had to make arrangements and could not put off decisions. Al and I had spoken many times about our wishes. We both wanted to be cremated rather than buried, our ashes scattered somewhere meaningful. Since we were avid sporting clay shooters, we joked that we would load our ashes into shotgun shells and break some clays with them.

We never had trouble discussing that kind of thing. We had both lost our parents and knew the difficulty of such decisions if you didn't know the last wishes of the deceased.

Even when you did know exactly what someone wanted, some details and choices remained to organize, implement, and resolve.

Before I could make anything happen, the Greensboro medical examiner had to release Al. In order to do so, she needed to examine him to determine cause of death and possibly perform an autopsy. She called me at the hotel to clarify some medical issues. Yes, he had high blood pressure and he took medication for it. Yes, he took other medications.

I called Al's doctor and had him call her. In the meantime, I took pictures of the pill bottles Al packed in his luggage and, hoping to clear things up and speed up the process, texted them to her. It did, and thus we could avoid an autopsy. She proclaimed the official cause of death "natural." Whether a heart attack or blood clot, I didn't feel the need to know. The result stayed the same.

It all took some time, and nothing about it felt "natural."

We waited and went downstairs to the hotel restaurant for a late breakfast and Paula's arrival. Her shuttle pulled up to the entrance, and she stepped off. She sported a large backpack and looked exhausted. Her flights from Hawaii had taken more than fourteen hours, and she hadn't slept since my call.

In the next few hours, her fatigue became more evident. We ordered breakfast and caught her up on the morning's developments. I had some decisions to make, but not immediately, and we all needed distraction. Luckily, the National Football League offered a great big one, available right where we sat.

The restaurant and bar area had multiple television sets within view. We sat at a corner booth that had a great line of sight to a TV no matter where in the booth you sat. It was Sunday, January 21, 2018, when the New England Patriots played the Jacksonville Jaguars at 3 PM, Eastern Standard Time. Al and I had planned on watching the televised game at noon, Nevada time, with Vern and Mary in our Las Vegas condo, but here we were. By then, the Patriots had built their dynasty, and every other NFL team and fan base hated them. There in North Carolina, New England Patriots haters surrounded us, providing just about the best distraction we could have hoped for.

We ordered snacks and drinks and watched as Paula—not exactly a football fan and carrying a big excuse—melted into the booth. She hadn't slept for more than twenty-four hours and ran on pure adrenaline but managed to watch the entire game without falling asleep.

The four of us watched the Patriots score fourteen points in the fourth quarter to beat Jacksonville and earn a spot in the Super Bowl. Yet again.

When the game ended, I noticed a text on my phone with a picture of a large group of our friends gathered around our seats at Gillette Stadium. They seemed to tell me that they were with me in spirit, and I felt their love and their loss all the way from Foxboro, Massachusetts.

Friends give thumbs up and number ones at a New England Patriots game in Foxboro, Massachusetts. They are, from left, Mark Johnson, Elizabeth Marble, Jen Johnson, Laura Marble, Angie Prescott, and Gary Suomala.

I would love to tell you that the Patriots went on to win the Super Bowl in honor of Al that year, but it didn't happen. They faltered to the Philadelphia Eagles when uncharacteristically, they allowed a touchdown with less than three minutes to play.

I wasn't crushed. I wasn't even annoyed. It didn't have the emotional impact it would normally command. My life had changed already. Or, should I say, I had.

I had to get him home. The thought began to consume me, overwhelm me. I called Jeff Cole, owner of Witty's Funeral Home in our hometown of Orange. We had met him several times through our business association. He asked me all the pertinent questions, and once I mentioned cremating Al, he suggested we could make arrangements to have it done in North Carolina, then ship his ashes home.

As much sense as it made, I found it difficult to process. I had to get beyond the realization that his physical self would never be back home. I took a little time to deliberate about that disquieting resolution. When I called Jeff back, I asked him to make the arrangements. The starkest realization of the decision meant leaving Greensboro without Al.

An emptiness fell over me like a black hole in my chest.

The next day, a shadow of myself, I flew home.

The Delta Ladies booked Paula, Vern, Mary, and me the first flight back to Bradley in the morning. I can't begin to describe the amount of compassion, support, and genuine affection complete strangers showed us in those three days. The two women from Delta stepped up at every moment with their emotional support and financial support from the airline.

Delta paid for everything: rooms, flights, and food vouchers. The wonderful people of the Marriot in Greensboro also stepped up. They didn't allow us to pay for food and drinks we consumed while watching the football game in the lounge, and those compassionate people took care of anything and everything we needed or wanted. And, of course, there are the individuals on the airplane whom I never had a chance to thank properly for their heroic efforts trying to save my husband's life plus the passengers and crew whose travel took them on an unexpected side trip to North Carolina.

As we checked out of the hotel that morning, I felt as if we left friends behind.

We had been at a memorial service for a family member during a snowstorm predicted to get worse as the day progressed.

The four of us—Big Brother, Little Brother, Mary, and I—decided to go to a nearby restaurant for a bite to eat and a cocktail. When we arrived, we found the restaurant closed due to the inclement weather. Across the street, we saw a daunting looking Chinese restaurant with a flashing *Open* sign that called to us.

We parked our separate cars in the vacant parking lot and headed into a dimly lit dining room, its bar running along the side wall. We chose four seats in the center of the bar and ordered mai tais. We had long since made it our life's mission to search out the best mai tai on the planet. Those were not the best ever, but it didn't prevent us from having more than we should. We ordered a few appetizers and engaged in conversation with the few snowmobile riders who stopped by for a quick drink or snack.

We spent a pleasant evening and could have stayed all night, but the weather worsened, and the time came to leave. The bartender handed the bill to Vern, who set it down beside him. Somehow, Al managed to pay the bill without Vern noticing, which made Vern very unhappy. He recited the unwritten, apparently unknown rule that whoever touches the bill first pays it. So, Vern pointed out, Little Brother touched it but Big Brother paid it, thus violating the rule. It all resulted in verbal sparring until we reached the parking lot and the snowbrushes came out.

Hours of snow buried our cars, vulnerable to the blizzard we hadn't paid attention to. But rather than use the brushes to clear off the vehicles, Big Brother and Little Brother used them as swords clacking, smacking, and thrusting at each other in their parking lot duel like a scene from a bad B movie. Having let it go on far longer that we should have, Mary and I broke up the skirmish and forced them to clean off the cars.

I drove the twenty-five miles home in whipping wind and occasional white-out conditions, all of us having been exceptionally irresponsible that evening.

I don't condone our behavior, but it's another of those lasting memories that leaves me smiling.

We arrived before the crowds at Greensboro's Piedmont Triad International Airport. I had walked through it before, of course, when we made the emergency landing, but none of it looked familiar. As we prepared to fly back to Bradley, my head spun with thoughts of how wrong it all felt, leaving that place, leaving Al behind.

In the two previous days, I never returned to the hospital nor called upon the morgue to see Al. The way everything had unfolded, the opportunity never presented itself, and, as Vern pointed out, what good could have come of it?

The final memory of my life with Al has him lying on a stainless-steel table covered with a thin white sheet as I hold his hand, a difficult and heartbreaking memory to take home. But I doubt that, had I seen him after that moment, I'd have any better memory.

Our boarding passes waited for us at Delta check-in. As we approached, two women came from behind the counter and gave me warm, no-holding-back hugs. It startled me. I had no idea who they were. They explained they had been there Saturday when we made the emergency landing. They heard what happened and had been praying for us. The exchange was genuine and endearing, and their hugs would have made Al proud.

Paula, Vern, Mary, and I continued to our gate. The attendant came directly to me and said, "I'm sure you don't remember but I was here when you came in." He also had been praying for us. Not long after, two white-collar, suitcoat-clad Delta executives checked in with us to see if we needed anything. They too had been praying for us.

I felt quite overwhelmed by the love coming from those wonderful people. I had never experienced anything like that from people I didn't know. It was pure, honest, emotional, and real. I sat somberly thinking I had become a real cynic about people in general. All the horrible stories take center stage. Every night, newscasts bombard us with them, newspapers overflow with them, and social media has exploded with instantaneous reports of pure evil.

I decided right then not to allow cynicism to manipulate me anymore. I would not let horrible people in the world overshadow all the amazing, caring, and loving people who far outnumber them.

We headed home. Although it really wasn't home anymore. What had made it a home was gone. I was left with a house with twenty-eight years of memories and much needed repairs. I had a business to run and a dog to take care of. Truth be known, the dog would take care of me. Animals are quite intuitive, and Randy sensed the gravity of the situation from the moment I picked him up from the kennel where we had left him. He immediately fell into a state of mourning, and I could see it in his eyes. I worried that it would be too much for him, a twelve-year-old Lab and Setter mix showing signs of slowing down.

He stayed by my side at home and at work, I can only guess, as much for me as for himself.

A splendid day for a ride, nearly cloudless and just cool enough to deem leather jackets necessary. Jackie, Jerry, Al, and I rambled along Route 26 in New Hampshire, formerly named Coös Trail, towards Dixville Notch where we took a short break.

    Helmet in hand, Al stood on the side of the road staring over Lake Gloriette at the grand structure known as The Balsams. A red roof shimmered in the lake's reflection amid autumn mountain colors. His long, slightly gray hair gathered in a ponytail reached below his shoulders, a doo rag covering the balding spot on the top of his head. He was at peace— in his element—in those surroundings.

    As he turned to set his helmet down on his motorcycle, he pointed to climbers ascending Tabletop Rock. Fascinated by

Chris and Al's bikes rest at a frequent stopping spot across from Lake Gloriette, New Hampshire, with the Balsams behind the lake on Route 26 through Dixville Notch.

their skilled movements, we watched. We didn't feel the need to speak as we simply absorbed our surroundings.

Both a complicated and simple person, Al loved the beauty of nature, the simplicity of silence, and the solidarity of family and friends. His love was unconditional, his loyalty unquestionable, and his aid always available. Al loved a good conversation, but when someone presented opposing political ideas for debate, he couldn't keep his cool. It infuriated him if he found litter during a walk through the woods. And he struggled with the thought of not having enough time to do all the things he wanted to do in his life.

That may be why he had a difficult time accepting the fact that he was losing his hair.

He had beautiful light brown hair that hid the oncoming gray quite well. As long as I had known him, he sported a goatee and mustache, neither of them hiding the gray. The issue really arose when he started to lose the hair on top of his head. The thinner it got on top, the longer he let it grow in the back.

He wore a ponytail for a year or so before I brought up the idea of shaving his head completely. Not that I minded the ponytail. I just thought he would look good with a bald head. He resisted. I enlisted our hairdresser, Kara, to help me convince him to give it a try.

It posed a complex dilemma for him in many respects. I believe he felt that, if he shaved his head, he would give up his youth and acquiesce to getting older. Not until we pointed out that longer, thinning hair made him look older, did he agree to shave his head. Of course, the goatee and mustache had to stay, we all agreed.

Kara was thrilled to be the one to dispose of Al's hair. We created a little party out of the event. The result was stunning. For some time, I pictured how he would look without hair, but he looked even better than I imagined. The best part? He really liked the look. From then on, Al shaved his head a few times a week at home.

Al's new look inspired the women in his office to rub his head. It quickly—and a bit oddly—became a game for them. As soon as they realized he had a fresh shave, each one of them jockeyed to be first to rub his head. He relayed the stories to me when he got home from work. Sometimes the women nearly knocked each other over to get to him first.

I thought it was hysterical!

Normally, I guess the little office contest would sound strange, but the co-workers also played together on a women's rugby team.

I thought I was competitive!

The next time Al stood on the side of the road, helmet in hand and staring over Lake Gloriette, he wore a doo rag then to prevent sunburn on his clean-shaved head rather than as a coverup of his waning youth.

Most everyone had heard the news. My social media page blew up with sympathy messages, our business Facebook page did the same . . . the new Hallmark of condolences. Even more messages inundated Al's personal page.

Two local newspapers printed articles on his passing. Not only a local businessman, he also served on the town planning board, so he received more attention than most. The radio station where we frequently advertised included it in its news. But word of mouth really spread the news. I got messages from as far away as Las Vegas by day two. The impact Al had on people he met, even if only for a moment, lasted. I always described him as the schmoozer compared to my reserved and shy personality when meeting new people. Al thrived on it.

NO MORE HELLOS

"How have you been?" you ask of me, and my reply is brief.
"I've been OK. I keep busy." Your smile shows some relief.

"It's been too long. Let's meet at Tea when schedules coincide."
To be polite, I do agree. I might as well have lied.

Away you walk. At peace you'll be. You think I'm moving on.
You do not know what you don't see: my motivation's gone.

I try to smile, I want to flee. My heart gives me away.
And every breath I take, I plead, "No more hellos today."

So please don't take it personally. There's something you must know.
The part of me you cannot see I will refuse to show.

It hurts too deep and painfully to let my grief show through.
Time will be my remedy. There's nothing you can do.

Nearly three months after Al died, drowsy but unable to sleep in the early morning of April 17, 2018, I lay in bed, and I wrote my first poem. I know—not because I have such a good memory, but—because I wrote the poem using an app on my cell phone, which recorded the exact date and time—12:32 AM—that I began. Swirling in my head as I lay there, the words just waited to be grabbed mid-air and put in order on paper—or in that case, cell phone.

I titled the poem "Distance." I did very little rewriting from the original except to add the last two stanzas the following day because I didn't want anyone to think that I planned to do anything drastic. Or maybe I wanted to remind myself that I had more to do before we could continue our journey together. Writing poems became a coping mechanism, a way to express my grief other than crying or sometimes doing both at once.

In the passing months, I wrote a short rhyming story about a little boy sad because his Dad has to work instead of taking him fishing. Big Al comes along and gives the boy a bear hug to cheer him up and to explain that his Dad must be sad, too.

I don't know exactly where the idea for the story came from, other than Al gave the best hugs in the world, but my sister-in-law Mary prodded me to write children's stories.

I enjoyed the writing process. It was fun, like having Al sitting there beside me as I wrote, and I saw it as therapy. But once I finished the story, I needed pictures. By then I already had an idea in my mind of what Big Al would look like. I saw him as a big, cuddly bear with a striking resemblance to Al.

I began to draw first with a graphite pencil, then colored pencils, then watercolor paints. I knew that, if I wanted to capture the attention of a child, especially my great-nieces and great-nephew, I would need bold, bright colors, so I transferred my drawings to the computer and created them there in vivid primary colors.

At the next family dinner, I brought my first draft copy of *A Big Al Bear Hug* children's story to get reactions. Mostly I got tears from the adults on seeing the resemblance to Al. Tears confused the kids who had already begun to forget about Al. In general, I got a good response. As the kids were quite young, I felt it more important than ever to continue the process, even if just to keep Uncle Al's memory alive in their world.

For the next seven months, I hardly left my bedroom. In May, 2019, seventeen months after Al passed away, I decided to renovate and remodel the house we had neglected for many years. With Mary's help, I drew up a plan. I elected to knock down the wall between my kitchen and living room, turn the three-season deck into a four-season family room with a bar, and remove the kitchen door altogether. I got an estimate and a timeline of between six and eight weeks.

I vacated everything from the affected areas by stuffing all furniture and possessions into the only room on the first floor not undergoing renovation. I planned to live upstairs while work progressed. I brought up chairs, a microwave, small refrigerator, and table for my laptop and printer to the bedroom. And there I stayed.

Almost every morning, the construction crew showed up, pounding, cutting, and hammering away. I barely heard a sound. I wrote and I drew. I immersed myself into the new world of children's stories with Big Al as my main character. And Bear Hug Books was born.

The six-to-eight-week renovation timetable came and went. It would take more time, they told me. A little more than six months and three contractor vacations later, they finished my refurbishing, and I had completed *A Big Al Bear Hug*, written and illustrated six more children's stories, including *The Case of the Missing Cooler*, designed and laid out a coloring book, and began to write this book. I also wrote some poems.

Not all the stories and poems are published. Some I have kept aside as I decide if I want them to see the light of day.

Some secrets remain.

RENOVATIONS

I make my plans. At every turn, I think, What would you do?
From my decisions, I will learn how much has come from you.

But while it is that I will make some choices that you would,
from my position you can't take for granted that I should.

It only shows how close we were in taste and property,
clearly shown by debt incurred when we spent happily.

I'll change things up. Some you'll approve. Others will make you cringe.
Your bear lamp I will have to move. That may give you a twinge.

*If that's the case, then let me know. I'll wait to hear from you—
any sign you want to show that you remember too.*

The contractors accomplished the job on my house just as I imagined it. Some of my choices strayed from Al's taste, but I think he would love it just the same. I couldn't bring myself to throw out his bear lamp, even though it doesn't fit with my new décor. That lamp was part of his life before he ever met me.

I hadn't always wanted to be a writer, although I always loved to write. I never seemed to choose my professions. They chose me, just as writing did after I lost Al.

In order to generate some spending money, as a child of eleven I found myself working in my grandfather's restaurant washing dishes and cleaning bushels of clams for steaming and serving. My grandfather prided himself on serving the cleanest and freshest steamed clams around. To accomplish that goal, I couldn't rush the long, arduous process, and I couldn't always remove every bit of sand without damaging the clams. It took hours, and you can bet that if anyone complained about dirty steamers, I heard about it. Even so, as diners' dirty dishes returned to the kitchen for washing, my grandfather periodically checked the bowls of clam broth they used to dip their clams to see if an unacceptable amount of sand had settled in the bottom of a bowl. He was very thorough.

Eventually I became prep cook, then fry cook and line cook. I was good at it, and I enjoyed it. My very demanding

Chris's grandfather Vern Johnson Sr. presides at the bar in his restaurant.

grandfather taught me how to do things the right way. I learned how to tend bar, wait on tables, control inventory, and place orders, but most of all, he taught me how to please the customers. There were Mike, the piano playing whiskey drinker, and his friend Pete, a beer-and-brandy guy with a handlebar mustache. Ed, a school bus driver, loved the twenty-five-cent draft beer. A host of regular customers found solace at the bar.

Though a stickler for perfection, my grandfather was a compassionate and quietly generous man. He never boasted about his many acts of kindness towards family, friends, and strangers. He had a profound impact on my life and on so many others'.

My whole family worked at Grandpa's restaurant at some point or another. My mother and sisters waited tables, my father sometimes tended bar, and my brother and I worked in the kitchen together.

Saturday nights meant big doings when the dinner rush preceded live music in the back room fitted with a service bar, stage, and dance floor. The Alley Cats, the most popular of bands, comprised three women in their late sixties wearing leopard print latex pants playing guitar, drums, and keyboard. Of the same ilk, the audience preferred mixed drinks like Grasshoppers, Seven and Seven, and Sombreros. Loyal customers all, but we lost them fast, mostly due to natural causes: not a sustainable business plan.

Only I stayed in the business and made it my career. I never had an interest in going to college, although I did take a one-year course in computer programming to appease my father. I remained working during that year of school because I didn't want to lose any momentum, I felt comfortable in the kitchen, and the money was always good.

Back in the seventies and eighties, few women worked in a restaurant kitchen. Almost everywhere I worked, I was the first or one of the first females to break through the male-dominated workforce. I suppose my competitiveness really came in handy there. Remembering everything my grandfather had taught me, I eventually worked my way up to chef.

I worked as a cook, then chef, twenty-six years or so into my late thirties.

I decided to leave the restaurant business for several reasons. Al worked a Monday-through-Friday job, and I worked nights and weekends, so we didn't have much of a social life. We wanted one. Also, my body—especially my hips and knees—constantly reminded me that it had an expiration date. The restaurant business is a brutal master.

I went straight from cooking to selling as I accepted a job as outside sales representative for one of my food distributors. I visited restaurants, schools, and hospitals to sign up new customers and provide customer service. It was a good fit. I knew the products, as I had been using them for years, and I knew the rigors of kitchen work. Not my ideal job, but it sufficed for about ten years and then gave way to my becoming an entrepreneur with our own retail sporting goods store.

Choices I made in my school years largely determined my work life, and I regret none of those choices. I understood early that my path would not conform to what society seemed to deem necessary, namely a college degree culminating in a so-called white-collar job.

I earned pretty much straight A's through fifth grade. I loved school and did well at it, but as I started to comprehend the dynamics of my home life, they affected me in ways that I didn't understand. In the early years I was largely shielded from the extent of my parents' torrents, but by the time I reached sixth grade, I became an angry child. Even though I lost my enthusiasm for school, I managed to attain passing grades, although my parents did not appreciate the margin for passing some of my classes. Somehow, they never seemed to notice my many absences as the years went by.

I built a wall around myself, a shield to keep me from being affected by those around me, including my neighborhood friends. I became the person who sits at the edge of the party, as I went through the motions, not participating in my own life. I disliked being surrounded by people either in the classroom or in public. I felt I had nothing in common with kids my age, most of whom seemed to live carefree lives. Perhaps I resented that they seemed so unencumbered.

One of my closest friends once said to me, after I uncharacteristically relayed a story of my parents fighting, "I wish my parents would fight, it's always so boring around here, nothing ever happens." I remember getting angry about her flippant reaction, although in her defense, she knew nothing of my home life.

I began to pull away, comfortable with only my own company.

As I reached my teenage years, I did anything to avoid being at home. In eighth grade, I took an after-school typing class at the nearby high school. I wasn't interested in typing. I had no desire to become a secretary or journalist or any other profession that required typing. I just didn't want to go home after school. Taught by Ralph Zona, we learned on old-fashioned typewriters as we keyed in cadence to his vocal prompts: f, space; j, space; d, space . . .

It was 1974, and society was beginning to accept the fact that women could be something other than office workers or teachers or nurses, but old habits die hard. Society saw typing as an important skill for a young woman to master, so my parents had no objections. What they didn't know was that it gave me access to the senior high school a full year before

I became a freshman, a crucial development if I wanted to pursue my new favorite pastime: smoking pot.

Drugs hadn't reached the lower grades in my town in the early seventies, but they ran rampant in the high school. If I had money, I could get anything I might want: marijuana, angel dust, cocaine, speed. You name it. It was available. Working in my grandfather's restaurant in the summer and on weekends afforded me enough funds. Even pressured by my peers, I seriously feared trying hard drugs. I wanted only pot and booze. Maybe I understood how easily I might let drugs take over my life. I don't know, but I did allow pot and booze to assist me in my socialization. The only time I felt really comfortable around other people was when I was buzzed or drinking.

I never went stoned to junior high school, but I can't say the same about high school. I arrived purposely late to the bus stop so I could walk the two miles to school, stopping partway through the woods to smoke a joint and arrive at school fashionably late.

The Shrewsbury school system burst at the seams in the seventies. Because of the large influx of students that year, the school committee had to make a choice. It voted to add multiple trailers to the grounds to serve as classrooms, but they didn't sufficiently accommodate the increased number of students who came into the school in 1975, my freshman year.

The good fortune was mine. The committee concluded only a four-day school week would make it possible to educate all of us. Twenty percent of students had Mondays off, another twenty percent stayed home on Tuesdays, and so on.

Although we didn't have a choice, I happened to receive my preferred day off, Wednesday, two of my four high school years. Since we considered Fridays senior skip days, if you had Fridays off, everyone figured that you got screwed.

Not everyone who skipped school on Friday was a senior, however, as I can attest. I didn't always cut school on Fridays, but many weeks in my four years, I attended classes only three days a week. Luckily for me, school came easy, so I could pass every course I took accept one: calculus. I had chosen it as an elective because I loved math, so when I failed, I simply chose a different course to take its place.

It's not that I didn't like learning. I liked to do algebra and geometry homework for fun. I finished the full year's curriculum only months into the school year, so my math teacher had no issue with me skipping a few classes. Considering that I had no plans to go to college, I learned to work the system to my advantage.

Only our Shrewsbury High School Class of 1979 went the entire four years with a four-day school week. When I graduated in May of 1979, I already worked in the career I would stay with for more than two decades.

Smoking pot helped get me through my high school years. It calmed me as life around me seemed out of my control. By the time I turned twenty years old, though, I no longer felt the need to self-medicate with marijuana. I grew comfortable in my career and became more confident as an adult.

I had to make more arrangements. I had to plan a party, not a wake and a funeral, but a *party* that would make Al proud, another one of the details we previously discussed. I suppose the socially acceptable term would be a celebration of life. I would have to observe some present-day proprieties, I decided, but I chose to keep them to a minimum.

I learned it could take up to two weeks before I received Al's ashes, but I didn't want to wait that long to have his Memorial. As much as I wanted him present, I didn't want to immerse myself in that process for an extra week. My brother called the local American Legion Hall, a smaller venue than I wanted, and booked it for the coming Saturday. The larger local hall I preferred had recently closed its doors. The Legion would be fine, I thought. I chose the caterer because Al and I once attended a small buffet he set up for one of our merchants group meetings. His food and setup impressed us both, and we thought him a very pleasant person. Ironically, the funeral home that would receive Al hosted that merchants' meeting.

My family never left my side. For the next few days, we looked through hundreds of photos to choose just the right ones for the requisite slideshow. We created and ordered thank-you cards I should send following the celebration-of-life party, finalized the menu with the caterer, and spoke with the bar manager to make sure of a sufficient supply of bourbon. We gathered necessary items to bring it all together, including a hat, flask, snowbrush, and cigar.

We were ready for Saturday.

At least we thought we were.

At noon, on Saturday the funeral home called. Al had arrived. He had made it home in time for his party.

I started to cry. I felt as if an angel from above took matters into its own hands.

I was shaking as Paula and I arrived at the funeral home. I gave Jeff a huge hug and thanked him profusely. I picked out a wooden box for Al's ashes. He would not have wanted anything other than wood. I wished I could have hugged everyone involved in getting him home so quickly. It meant the world to me, and Al would not have enjoyed missing a party.

We posted hours from three to six that afternoon. We planned to meet the rest of the family at two to get things set up before people began to arrive. But we hadn't accounted for flowers. I received some deliveries at home, and we brought them with us, but as it turned out, we didn't need to. The florist van had already shown up packed with gorgeous arrangements, and we had to make room for them.

The first guest showed up forty-five minutes early. About fifteen feet inside the doorway, we set up a receiving line, one of the proprieties I acknowledged. For the next three hours, the line extended out the door and wound through the parking lot in New England January cold in a long, heartwarming, exhausting process. So many people loved him—people he worked with recently and twenty years before, people he knew from sporting clays, town politics, the gun club, customers from our store, Patriots football games, and of course, family.

Al's legacy lives in the hearts of those who loved him, in the simple joy he spread to others, and on display at his memorial: the silliness of a snow brush, the hilarity of hats, the fun of the flask, and the serenity of a cigar.

Friends old and new stopped in to have a drink in memory of Al. The hall wasn't big enough. The crowd poured into the adjacent, private bar section, some people choosing to use the side entrance, bypassing the long line. Most everyone got through the line by six o'clock. If anyone arrived after that, they would have to come find me in the crowd.

Someone passed out hats from the box we brought from home. People smiled and laughed as they recalled story after story of Al. For a moment, I sat watching, happy tears in my eyes. "Switch," I heard someone yell, the scene fulfilling exactly what Al and I had talked about, just what he said he wanted.

Someone handed me a bourbon.

We finished the evening back at our house. I set Al on the table we transformed into a bar, and we toasted him all night.

Some of us were intoxicated, and some of us were exhausted, but I couldn't tell the difference.

Day Eight, Sunday—the day of rest. I woke up. I didn't want to, but I did. There would be a lot of such bleak mornings to come. Paula planned to stay with me a while longer, and my brother and Mary only an hour away checked in frequently. Suspecting I couldn't count on too many more days with our dog Randy, I snuggled on the couch with him and did nothing.

When something tragic happens, you react. You do what needs to be done, whatever it takes, however long it takes. When it's resolved, you think you will have time to process everything, get it straight in your head. As I'm sure many people before me have learned, the previous week was just the beginning. The amount of paperwork following the death of a loved one is staggering. Life insurance, health insurance, home-owners' insurance, Social Security filings, credit cards, bank accounts, bills, registrations, and more, and more.

And that just concerned the house. I had the store to deal with, too. It all became so overwhelming that, in place of feeling sad and mourning the death of my husband, I began to feel angry and resentful about what he left me to deal with. And then, in turn, while also feeling sad, I felt guilty about feeling angry.

Is that the way it's meant to be? Is that what I'll remember?

They say that you shouldn't make big decisions during times of stress, but they don't tell you how long you should wait. I closed the store eleven months after I lost Al. I hadn't planned on closing but, it just wasn't fun anymore, and I was tired. I lost Randy two months earlier. He loved going to the store for ten years as he greeted every customer and waited for treats from his favorites. Once he was gone, the decision became easier.

I held a going-out-of-business sale and then an auction to get rid of leftover products and equipment. It was bittersweet, but it was time. I decided I would retire from the workforce and rent out the building for some income.

While we owned the store, we inadvertently created a routine—not something we consciously planned, but it fell into place just the same.

By the time Saturday nights rolled around, Al and I needed to decompress. As it turned out, so did our friends Laura and Gary. It started innocently enough. They stopped by the store at closing time on Saturday nights, and we had a few drinks to unwind. Sometimes we stayed there for hours enjoying the fact that none of us had to work the next day. After a while, we realized we should probably change the location for our gatherings, maybe have a little food available as we consumed beer, bourbon, Fireball, and cigars: a familiar theme. Sometimes in good weather, we went to their house and had a fire in the backyard. Other times, they came to our house. Saturday night decompression is still a thing, one of the few routines in my life that hasn't changed. In a life where almost everything has changed, one that I most appreciate and value.

Chris and Madelyn celebrate Madelyn's tenth birthday in 2018.

Laura has a daughter Madelyn who quickly became our surrogate child. She is a sweet girl with a huge heart. The family also belongs to our White Mountain camp cohort. For a young girl, Madelyn had already endured too many losses in her life. Two of her school friends died not long before in a house fire, and her father, to whom she was devoted, passed away unexpectedly. I particularly worried about how Al's death would affect her. She was nine years old—so much loss for someone so young. But Madelyn has inspiring resilience, incomparable compassion, and friendship I most cherish. She consoled me, hugged me, made me smile every chance she got, and with grace beyond her years, does to this day. I am grateful to have her in my life.

PROGRESS

I take a step into the light,
weights upon my feet.
The brightness blinds me as I fight—
Progress in defeat.

A quiet whisper from a friend,
the subtle boost a feat.
Will I make it to the end?
Progress so discreet.

A rush of thoughts can make my day
or send me to retreat.
A laugh, a tear goes either way.
Progress bittersweet.

Darkness is a pulling force,
solace so replete,
dangerous at this mid course.
Progress obsolete.

Yet again I lift the weight
still heavy on my feet.
A painful struggle is my gait.
Progress incomplete.

There is no other measure
except my own heartbeat—
my life without your pleasure.
Progress is deceit.

My marriage to Al was nothing like my parents' marriage. In fact, it often surprised me that—not having the best models for the endeavor—I could function at all in a relationship. However chaotic my parents' union, they really did love each other in their own way, right until the end. The obstacles were just too overwhelming.

I can count on less than one hand the number of serious verbal altercations Al and I had in our thirty-year relationship. Not to say we didn't have disagreements or misunderstandings, but contentious clashes occurred very few and far between. We grew adept at recognizing days when communication turned futile, and we'd agree to shelve discussion for a later time.

I credit our success much more to Al than to me. He was born to be a husband: attentive, humorous, and genuine. He taught me how to say, "I love you." I didn't hear those words very often as I grew up, not in the early years anyway. No one verbalized it, although I knew my parents loved me.

Every day, Al told me that he loved me and prompted me to tell him. It took some getting used to, but after a time, I didn't need prompting. Even though he said it every day, he was never insincere, never matter-of-fact about it. And I never took it for granted. That could be why what I'm about to recall hurt me as much as it did.

We had recently celebrated our twenty-eighth wedding anniversary, and I felt very happy and content. Al and I were having a normal conversation when I interjected the notion that we had the "perfect marriage."

His extemporized response both surprised and deflated me. He spoke just three words that would haunt me well after his death. He said, "Well, not perfect."

I was shocked, physically and emotionally paralyzed, and on the verge of tears. As he realized what he had said, he tried to backtrack by explaining that nothing is ever "perfect."

But it was too late. The words already had tattooed themselves on my heart. Trying to understand what I had just heard, I walked away. The fact that he replied so quickly, as if he had the response already on his mind, sent me into a depression-like state that would last for many days.

Trying not to show the hurt, I went through the motions, but I don't think I succeeded.

I suppose he was right. Nothing is ever perfect. I know that I certainly wasn't. But having lived through a tumultuous and volatile upbringing, I believe our relationship was close enough to perfect, even at our worst times.

I'm pretty sure Al regretted that statement, although we never talked about it again.

Not in this lifetime.

I rolled over and reached for the empty space in our king-sized bed. Given what I learned that day, I found it impossible to sleep. How much could I believe, if any?

I awoke that morning looking forward to a new and unfamiliar experience. Skeptical, I found it surprising that I had agreed to see a medium—a psychic as some would call her. A reserved person by nature, I felt nevertheless desperate to connect with Al.

He had passed away twenty-three months before.

I was the third of four people scheduled for a reading. As the second emerged with wet eyes and a dazed expression from the private room, I began to second guess my open-mindedness. *Keep things to yourself,* I told myself. *Don't say anything that could give her a hint of who you are or what you might be seeking,* the cynic in me demanded.

Her name is Joanne Collins. I introduced myself, first name only, and sat across from her in the cramped little room. We sat at a small white table next to a window overlooking the side yard of my friends' old farmhouse.

She didn't waste any time.

She glanced away, her face turned up and to the right as if looking at a lamppost light. When her gaze came back to me, she asked if I was in the process of relocating or had recently relocated.

I felt a bit confused by the question but told her no, I hadn't moved and had no plans to move.

"That's strange," she said. "She keeps saying 'moving.'"

"Who is saying that?" I asked.

"Your mother," she replied.

I immediately thought back to a few months earlier when the idea of participating in a reading had birthed. I had attended a psychic fair at the majestic Mount Washington Hotel in New Hampshire's White Mountains. Al and I had always wanted to stay there but never got around to it, so when my sister and a friend asked if I wanted to attend the psychic fair, I said yes.

Mostly, the hotel itself interested me along with the speakeasy housed in the bowels of the structure. I also admit that I had become increasingly curious about the idea of having a reading with a medium.

As we entered the ballroom and the fair, I felt immediately drawn to a dark-haired woman seated at a corner table on the right side of the room. Busy, she had a steady line of eager souls desiring her capabilities.

As time grew short, I kept watching for an opportunity to confer with her. My friend Shelly stepped in and procured me the final reading of the day.

I sat for a twenty-minute session with Maria. My mother came through in that reading, too. In the short time we had, the magnetic medium relayed plausible information to me. She allowed me to think it conceivable that I indeed communicated with my mother, who had died nine years before.

"Well, I'm not moving," I told Joanne. "I just remodeled my house. But my sister just moved in with me."

"Oh," Joanne replied as she turned her head up slightly and smiled. "That must be it."

After a slight pause, Joanne resumed.

"She just said 'Well, this should be fun.'"

I couldn't help but chuckle. My mother would say that.

During that session with Joanne, my mother went on for another ten minutes or so about my sister and me, describing our relationship, how different we were and yet very much the same.

Through Joanne, my mother said I was grounded, that I had my space and was happy to stay there. Joanne channeled my mother as describing my wandering sister with "one toe in the ground."

Most of what Joanne related struck me as accurate and compelling. A few of her comments seemed cloudy and confusing, though, their meaning remains to be seen.

The topic shifted from my sister to my mother. Joanne said my mother wanted me to know many things, including things about her childhood we had only speculated about.

We never really knew what happened to her as a child, but through conversations over the years and stories she told—the bits and pieces that remained in her memory after the treatments—I assumed her alcoholic father had physically abused her.

Joanne glanced up again, a sign of more communication. She turned to me and said, "She wants to know why the book isn't done."

For just a few moments, I was speechless. I had never mentioned anything about my books to Joanne. She couldn't have known, especially not about the book I suspected my mother referred to through Joanne. Only four other people knew about it.

When I attended my reading with Joanne, I had begun to write this book. I originally intended to center my account around Al and the day that he died, but as it developed, I also decided to include recollections of my parents, siblings, and childhood. "Which book?" I responded.

Joanne looked up and murmured, "She said it should be done by now."

I gathered my thoughts and told her I had changed the scope of my book. I was rethinking how to go about it.

"Oh, okay," Joanne said, channeling my mother.

"Why? Is she upset about it?" I asked.

"No, she thinks it is a great idea. She thinks it could help people."

With another glance and pause, Joanne's expression changed slightly. "She's telling me 'rape.' She says she was raped when she was—I think she's saying fifteen years old. No. Fourteen. She was raped when she was fourteen."

Confused, I said, "Well, I know something happened to her when she was a child, but I wouldn't call it rape. We always assumed that she was abused, but I wouldn't characterize it as rape."

"She's telling me that you don't know about this. She is also saying 'uncle.' I don't know whose uncle, if it's her uncle or your uncle," she went on.

Joanne relayed a vivid description. A man raped my mother beside the train tracks when she was fourteen years old. She said the rapist, whom she referred to as Uncle, wore a black hat turned backwards on his head.

"Did I know this man?" I asked Joanne.

"No," she promptly answered as she continued to channel my mother.

If a legitimate account, I could believe one of my grandfather's alcoholic brothers, none of whom I met, may have sexually abused her. I had heard all his brothers had a drinking problem.

I remember thinking it made sense. I no longer have reason to believe that my grandfather physically abused my mother, though I had a staunch conviction that neither he nor her self-absorbed mother had the capacity to protect her. Surely, I further conjecture, she would not have confided in her brother. She was alone.

Now she wants me to write about it, I thought. *Why else would she want me to know what happened to her as a child? Why else would she say that the book would help people?*

Joanne interrupted my chain of thought. "Is there anything else you want to know? Anything that you want to ask?"

I saw my time dwindling, so I said, "Yes. Does she ever get to see Al?"

"I'll ask her to get him." She surprised me with that answer. I didn't know I could just ask to speak with someone.

She told me my mother, a force who wanted to be the center of attention, did not want to give up the spotlight.

I had no trouble believing that, and I had heard it before. At my inaugural reading in New Hampshire, Maria told me the same thing.

The pause lasted a bit overlong.

When Joanne finally spoke, she said, "He's pissed."

What did I do? I immediately thought. *Maybe my remodeling of the house displeased him.*

"He's pissed," she said again.

She told me he repeated the word *dinner* a couple of times.

Somewhat relieved, I couldn't help but smile. *So much for keeping things to myself,* I thought. The obvious explanation for his comment? Only three people on the planet would understand it. Al and I once discovered a place in Las Vegas called Capo's, a combination restaurant and speakeasy that, apparently, uses Al Capone's recipe for tomato sauce. On a previous stay, we tried to get in for dinner one night which involved having to circle around the back of the dimly lit building, walk into a dark vestibule, and press a buzzer.

After a moment, a small sliding door opened, and a gruff male voice asked, "What do you want?"

Al requested a table for two.

The door opened into a bustling room with red velvet wallpaper, leather-clad booths, and a long ornate bar down the side wall. Mirrors along the wall reflected the room and the people in it back onto themselves. Packed, the place had not a barstool or table available.

The maître d' said hours might elapse before we could get a seat, so we left, although vowing to return, next time with reservations.

A few days before we left for Las Vegas, we made reservations for four at Capo's for the following Tuesday night. We never made it because of the detour to Greensboro, North Carolina, and Al was pissed!

Before she continued, I explained a little to Joanne.

"He came back for a while," she said.

Then, during a peculiar scene for me, I watched her having a short disagreement with my deceased husband, turning her face up and saying, "Well, that's not a while."

She told me he had come back just for a minute or so, but that the "pull was too strong."

She held her right arm out straight and pointed on an angle to her right.

"You were there," she said as she pointed, "but he could only see part of you." With her fingers, she traced out a rectangle so I could visualize what he could see: just the top part of my body. She could not possibly have known in advance that the airplane galley counter concealed the lower part of my body. I hadn't told her about those fraught moments on the plane.

I didn't need more convincing. I had already heard enough to believe she had contacted Al. When I first saw him in the airplane lavatory, his eyes were shut. If he saw me, it wasn't through the beautiful blue eyes he was born with.

"He's pissed," Joanne said once again. I had a fleeting thought: *How odd for a soul to be pissed off, a soul presumably living in the ultimate happy place.*

What now? "He wanted to surprise you," she said.

My inner cynic reappeared.

Joanne continued that Al had planned for us to renew our vows on that trip— not so much in a romantic way, but in a fun and silly way. She explained that, on an earlier trip to Las Vegas, we had seen a chapel and made jokes about renewing our vows—all true.

We once saw the White Chapel where Jon Bon Jovi got married and joked about doing that. But doesn't everyone? Or almost everyone?

The idea of actually renewing our vows in the White Chapel seemed completely out of character for Al, and she brought it up not long after I told her we were on our way to Las Vegas, thus sprinkling more doubt in my mind.

I asked her to ask him if he had told Vern and Mary about his plan. Joanne said, "No."

Strike three. I couldn't imagine him planning something like that . . . until much later, when I related the story to Paula. *Then*, three little words popped into my head . . . "Well, not perfect."

Could that exchange have bothered him as much as it did me? What could possibly remove all doubt about how he felt about me and our marriage than renewing our vows?

Goodbye, Cynic, I thought. *I'm sure you will find another way into my psyche soon.*

A few more curious things cropped up during my reading with Joanne. For example, she said my Dad was out golfing with his best friend in the best kind of afterlife I can imagine for Dad. She described his golfing buddy accurately as very short with gray hair. She said my mother always surrounds herself with her women friends, including her fun-loving sister-in-law Betty. She said they keep men at bay, although occasionally she connects with my father.

And she said Al wanted to tell me I was the best thing that happened to him, although I know it was the other way around.

Spirituality and skepticism have always gone hand-in-hand in my world. When I was younger, I was never curious enough to see where my spirituality would take me or what, if any, metaphysical boundaries exist. I have always believed in ghosts and, therefore, spirits. I have always believed that things happen for a reason, and, therefore, fate. And I have always believed that, as human beings we don't use the spiritual or metaphysical attributes bestowed upon us, so we don't necessarily know how to access those qualities.

Of the three female children in my family, only I — skeptical and maybe stubborn—refused until recently to explore the world of metaphysics. Both my sisters have maintained open minds about all aspects of spirit, including worlds of guardians, channeling, and otherworldliness. As children they shared an unusual incident, but their story is not mine to tell.

Were it destined for me to bear witness to their experience that same night, I might, too, have been more susceptible and less cynical about the empirically inexplicable. But, even then, I probably could have gone only so far before my father's practical side would prevail. I suppose that my recent life's events made the doorway to the mysterious more appealing. I found myself listening more to the idealistic influence of my mother as I began to develop an open mind and see where it might take me.

The first rune-stone reading I recall took place after Al passed away. We used Paula's personal set of Nordic runes.

Runes may serve as tools of divination in order to look at our spiritual needs and well-being, tools for inner guidance or even confirmation, if desired. I don't remember which runes I drew or which layout I chose, but I do remember the gist of the reading. It concerned loss, struggle, grief, and love.

I cried through the whole thing. In other words, it struck me as extremely pertinent and dead-on accurate. Of course, I had to do another reading to prove that it wasn't a fluke. I can't explain it, and I don't know how it works, but I can't ignore the relevance and aptness of the readings I receive. Paula gave me my own set of runes. I do my own readings when I have a question or concern or if I simply want guidance about something I should pay attention to.

Sometimes the runes tell me what I need to know, if not what I want to know, and their significance always registers as timely and introspective.

Paula also introduced me to angel cards, small rectangular cards each with a printed word and picture representing, for example, grace, strength, abundance, and more. I find it fascinating that I seem to pick the same twelve or so cards from the forty-five available, even though I shuffle and spread them and leave them face down.

The cards are meant to reflect conditions in one's life at the time of choosing or maybe some aspect of one's life requiring attention. I can draw cards daily, similar to reading a horoscope, but cards gear toward my life energy, not my zodiac sign, and only I can choose them.

I began reading runes and angel cards before I agreed to go to the White Mountains and before I agreed to see a medium, so I wasn't a complete virgin when it came to the metaphysical arts. I was inexperienced with a third-party conduit, however, and after my first figurative "ménage à trois," I *did* need a cigarette when it was over.

After the session with Joanne, I became more open to exploration of my inner soul and the souls that I surround myself with. They say that opposites attract. I submit that like-minded souls search out like-minded souls in this life and beyond—maybe not in the conventional sense of the term but in the familial sense. It's been said that we can't choose our family but maybe we choose each other well before we are physically born.

Have you ever met someone and liked them right away before even exchanging a word? Or passed someone on the street and shuddered, cold and ill at ease? I believe that, for the most part, we surround ourselves with familiar souls, and new souls dart in and out of our existence like hummingbirds searching for the perfect nectar. Some join the family while others move on.

My friend Sasha from the Petersham Gun Club asked me if it would be okay to hold a sporting-clays shoot in Al's memory. Money raised would send a young adult to the Massachusetts Junior Conservation Camp.

I thought it fitting in keeping with Al's support of the camp and everything taught there. I considered it a great opportunity to generate something good from our great loss.

We scheduled the event for July. The fliers went out to gun club members, and many social media shares publicized the shoot. The closer we got to the date, the more anxiety I had about it. I kept picturing another receiving line along with the exhaustion of smiling and telling people that I was "fine."

The night before the shoot I invited some friends to the house. I set up our shotgun shell reloader, and we each carefully placed Al's ashes into the hulls. We wrote our names on each of the shells to ensure we would each shoot the shell personally loaded. I kept thinking how much he would love it, because for as many times as he and I had joked about it, I couldn't assess its actual feasibility.

Nor had I fully considered the emotional impact of the process. When we finished loading shells, I reached for a bottle of bourbon, and we toasted Al again and again and again.

Morning came quickly—too quickly, and I wasn't ready for it. We stayed up way too late and drank too much bourbon. A hangover wouldn't lend itself to a day of shooting.

I wanted to go back to bed, but I knew that I didn't have that option. On the bright side, it looked like a beautiful day in the offing, a little too beautiful in fact. Intense July sun would shine from early morning until sunset.

I got to the club and got out of the truck. I could feel every pore of my body oozing the spirits from imprudence of the previous night. If I didn't stay hydrated, I would never make it. I chastised myself for recklessness, for putting myself into that state. I would just have to push through.

People began arriving—a lot of people. I hadn't talked to anyone about the sign-ups, so I didn't know what to expect. Sasha reached out to local businesses and individuals for donations to hold a raffle, proceeds to be added to the Junior Conservation fund. The clubhouse continued to fill with people and prizes. I spent the next hour telling people that I was "fine" and thanking them for coming.

When shooting began, I hung back for as long as I could. I didn't feel driven to complete the course. I wanted only to complete the task at hand: shooting my husband's ashes out of my shotgun. In my post-inebriated state, I feared I wouldn't hit any targets.

Normally, I am a very good shot, and the targets they had set that day were soft, set for novices in order to make it easy to hit the targets instead of the usual challenging course set for seasoned sporting clays shooters. We wanted to have fun and raise money for a good cause in Al's memory. I feared even more missing the clays and doing a disservice to Al's ashes.

The time came. My group consisted of friends from the previous night and a few others probably thankful they hadn't joined us the night before, as those of us who had been at the shell-filling gathering couldn't hide our physical discomfort.

I stepped into the designated shooting box. I called "Pull" so I could examine the targets for that station: it's called a show pair.

Chris loads her shotgun with a specially prepared twelve-gauge shell holding Al's ashes.

I loaded two shells, each with my name on them, into my shotgun. I took a deep breath and raised the gun to my shoulder.

"Pull."

I pressed the trigger twice to create two separate clouds of orange dust mingling with Al's ashes. I lowered my gun and cried.

We shared our special shells with others in the group. Each of us repeated the process, some crushing the targets, some not.

We all cried. We managed to get around the rest of the course, not shooting particularly well but enjoying it, nonetheless. I started feeling human again about halfway through when my instincts kicked in, and I finished with a strong surge.

Chris fulfills Al's wish as she shoots Al's ashes from her twelve-gauge shotgun.

photo by Mary Khory Whitelaw

Al always said, "It's better to start bad and finish strong than to start strong and finish bad."

We raised enough money to send four kids to camp, a resounding success. Al would be proud to know he played a part in the outdoor education of those young adults. The coup de grâce happened after lunch. My friend Dan offered his cannon for the event finale. I gave him some of Al's ashes, and he had it loaded and ready by the time we finished eating.

Everyone gathered down by the pond. I tried to say a few words, but they got stuck in my throat. I managed a "Thank you for coming" and prepared to light the fuse.

Dan instructed me on the proper way to approach and stand at the cannon. He told me it had a short fuse, so it would fire almost instantly.

I wanted to laugh, thinking of the irony in his comment. One of Al's favorite self-deprecating jokes characterized him as "four hundred pounds of dynamite with a three-inch fuse."

Dan was right. I lit the cannon and Al went immediately sailing across the pond.

During a beautiful and somber moment, the percussion of the cannon rippled through my entire body. It discharged whatever anxiety I had left, launching it across the pond in a cloud of tranquility.

*Leaving behind a cloud of tranquility,
the cannon launches Al's ashes across the pond.*

*As the pond claimed the essence of Al, so does the Snake River, Idaho,
three months later as Paula releases his ashes there.
As lonely rivers flow to the sea,
a small bit of Al hitches a ride on the Snake's tears
all the way to the Pacific Ocean where he rides the waves of eternity.*

Until Such Time Your Hand I Hold
an afterword by Christine Noyes
February 11, 2020 • two years, twenty-two days

On my newly revamped deck, a fresh lager in my glass, an Arturo Fuente cigar in hand, I sat in my well-padded chocolate-colored leather chair, the ottoman holding my weary legs two feet above the floor. Paula and I had just returned home from an eventful week in Florida visiting our great-niece Taylor and escaping the New England winter. I reflected on the array of activities we enjoyed, especially the firsts. My first time at Daytona Speedway feeling the thunder of cars rumbling past me during the longest Busch Clash race to date with an improbable winner who crossed the checkered flag with a crushed front end and a little help from his teammate. My first seafood boil. My first time in a metaphysical store. My first trip to St. Augustine. My first tattoo.

Al and I always talked about getting tattoos. He wanted a bald eagle clutching an American flag, while I leaned towards an infinity symbol with all our animals represented in five dog prints and one cat print. The tattoo turned into one more item that fell through the hole in his bucket.

The idea of a tattoo resurfaced as my intentions turned into a way of commemorating Al. At home I considered local tattoo parlors but hadn't made any commitments. While discussing our upcoming trip to Florida, Paula and I bandied about the notion of getting tattoos during the trip, but we never made any definitive plans.

On Saturday, Paula, Taylor, and I made plans to go to St. Augustine, a historic town—the first European settlement in North America. I had never visited, and Paula had only driven through. Several people, Taylor among them, advised us that we would love the city and should include it on our itinerary, which we made up as we went along.

Two days before, on Thursday, as Paula and I enjoyed a leisurely morning sitting on the patio of our hotel room in Daytona, we decided to do a rune reading. When Paula picked the Warrior Rune, whose symbol is an arrow, she mentioned that it might be the tattoo she would like to get—just a small arrow on her index finger, pointing forward. As we read the elements of the Warrior Rune, we came across the following:

> Patience is the virtue of this rune, and it recalls the words of St. Augustine that *the reward of patience is patience.*

Without hesitation, we picked up our cell phones and googled "tattoo shops in St. Augustine." Multiple choices popped up on the screen but only one we both agreed upon. We made the decision: if it were meant to be, we would each get a tattoo in St. Augustine.

Without any reservations, including both prior appointment and personal misgivings, Paula, Taylor, and I drove into the city on Saturday morning and headed directly to the tattoo parlor.

And so, it was meant to be. The busy shop could fit us in. We had to wait only a scant fifteen minutes.

Paula knew what she wanted scored on her finger, but I still contemplated my design as we signed waivers. My deliberation culminated in an infinity symbol, its line passing through a heart on the left and incorporating Al's name in cursive on the right. I had it scribed on my inside right wrist, where I can admire it daily.

Chris honors Al's memory in her first tattoo, a bucket list fulfillment experienced in St. Augustine, Florida.

As advertised and now indelibly etched in my mind and on my body, St. Augustine proved a great city for strolling and reveling in diversities of humanity.

We had a delightful week, full yet unhurried, exhilarating yet tranquil, and perfectly suited to our intentions.

So why did I now sit at home in my beautiful new space, fogged in with the remnants of my maduro-wrapped cigar, sinking into despondency?

I have come to realize that grief in many ways resembles the depression my mother dealt with every day of her life. Every high has a low, every good has a bad—at least for me. Chemical imbalance doesn't define my state. Rather situational imbalance depicts it.

Situational imbalance: how perfectly that describes my life after Al. I sit on a seesaw opposite no one, resting on the ground until I am distracted by a party, a dinner, a vacation. As I engage in activities, collective feelings of loss I hold inside slowly drift over to the other side of the seesaw to face me and lift me off the ground until I am balanced. As the distraction wraps up, feelings slowly return to my side of the beam to sink me.

Grief doesn't always wait for the conclusion of my distractions or efforts to deflect it. Sometimes grief demands to be included and sneaks over the fulcrum, inches back towards me, sometimes successfully reaching its home too soon, other times fended off for a bit longer.

Someone asked me if my feelings have been like this from the beginning, since Al died?

Well, no. For the first couple of years, I held my feelings close to my heart without allowing them to wander outside their residence. I didn't acknowledge their role on my beam. I didn't want to be lifted.

Progress so discreet.

But what would progress look like in my situationally unbalanced world? Do I conclude that I should stay distracted, keep my feelings on the other side of the beam for as long as I can, build a wall over the fulcrum to prevent them from ever returning?

To some extent, that's what I did with my childhood memories, some locked away forever. But here is the conundrum . . . I don't want to. I want to remember every single detail, good or bad, of my time with Al. I don't want to "get over it" or "move on." There is no such thing, and anyone who suggests that has never lost someone they truly love.

Progress is deceit.

I don't need to progress. I have reached my goal. I choose to embrace what's left—my grief, occasionally setting it aside for a little while but always welcoming it back into my soul, hugging it like an old tattered teddy bear, savoring it for what it represents: Love.

When I began writing my memoir, I did it just for me. I felt it my way of ejecting the pain from my heart. But, as with most therapeutic activities, the process taught me I needn't eject the pain. I should embrace it, celebrate it. If I didn't have the pain, I didn't have the love.

I never know what sight, sound, or smell will trigger my emotions. Grief mostly hits me without warning like the pop of a water bottle, as if to remind me that things can change in an instant.

Not long after Al died, I drove his Dodge Journey along a back road in our hometown when I heard the familiar pop, the sound you get when you stick the tip of your index finger inside your mouth and pluck the cheek.

I instantly began to cry and laugh at the same time.

Al kept a partially full plastic water bottle in the passenger seat cup holder. In colder months, the bottle collapsed. With the car heat on, the bottle warmed up to expand the plastic, causing it to make that popping sound.

After the sound startled me several times, I asked Al why he didn't throw the plastic bottle away. He explained that he had become accustomed to using it as a time reference when he drove to work, since it popped at almost the same spot in his travel every day. He found it somehow reassuring.

And then, so did I.

The bottle remained a comfort to me, a welcome companion in my routine days until its untimely demise, an accidental victim of the Massachusetts recycling laws.

During my reading with Joanne, she relayed that my mother thought my book could help people. I don't know about that. I can only hope that it might. I do know it has helped me tremendously, and I hope that my mother is proud of the result.

As for Al, I will continue to spend every day with him, whether through creation of my children's book series, my dreams, or my thoughts. He is the best part of me. *"Until such time your hand I hold, next to you as I sleep."*

And this I leave with you . . .

Don't hesitate to say "I love you."

Life can change in an instant. Be happy. Share happiness.

Listen to your heart, not your wallet.

Have dinner with your family. It may surprise you how much you enjoy each other.

Make peace with your regrets. Forgive yourself, but don't forget yourself.

Nurture your relationships with others, and the next time around will be easier.

And . . .

Always carry a hat, a flask, a snowbrush, and a cigar!

Al and Chris enjoy a summer day.

About the Author

You can't always plan where life will take you.

That certainly proved true for Christine Noyes. Growing up a tomboy in Shrewsbury, Massachusetts, she spent her youth building forts, playing sports, and enjoying the perceived innocence of the 1960s.

Without a clear vision of what her life should be, she went where she felt most comfortable: to the kitchen. At the age of eleven, she began her work life as a dishwasher in her grandfather's restaurant. She spent the next several decades reinventing herself, becoming an accomplished chef and then a sales representative, an entrepreneur, and eventually a writer and illustrator.

Chris never chose her professions. They chose her.

Few people say that going bowling changed their lives, but it did exactly that for Chris. She met the one person she never expected to meet, the man she calls her husband and soulmate, Al.

After marrying in 1989, they moved to Orange, Massachusetts, where, after Al's passing, Chris resides with thirty years of wonderful memories to keep her company.

When not at her keyboard, she enjoys her kitchen: back to her roots and love of cooking.

Acknowledgments

First and foremost, to my husband, Al: I want to thank you for the amazing life we shared. I knew we belonged together from the moment we met, and apparently so did you. But don't think you are off the hook for leaving me too soon and in such a dramatic fashion. We'll discuss that when next we meet. I love you.

Thank you, my sister-in-law Mary, for marrying my brother and convincing him that I am a cool person to hang out with. You and I became friends even before we became family and I couldn't have written *Close Enough to Perfect* without the encouragement and support from you and Vern. I am forever grateful for all you both do.

To my sister Paula: you inspire me every day to be the best person I can be, even on those days when I don't want to be. You see all my flaws and love me anyway. Your invaluable input for *Close Enough to Perfect* almost qualifies you to receive royalties for each sale . . . I said almost.

Thank you to my mother and father who made it all possible. I have always felt fortunate to have received the best parts of you both. I hope you take pride in what I have done with them.

To my grandfather: you gave me a work ethic and the inspiration for a career that I enjoyed. I thank you.

To my sister Pam and the rest of my wonderful family—nieces, great-nieces, nephews, great-nephew, aunts, uncles, and cousins—I appreciate the comfort and support you have all given me throughout my life, but especially during the most difficult period of losing Al. I mean, some of you are off-the-wall but that just makes it more fun!

To my camp cohort: it is astonishing to me how many remarkable people Al and I have surrounded ourselves with. And I say remarkable because they probably won't let me print "batshit-crazy." Jackie, Jerry, Kristy, Scotty, Laura, Gary, and Madelyn, you are my own personal cheering squad and you keep me grounded.

To Shelly, Kara, Artie, Marlene, Artie III, and the Friday Night Tea House crew: you keep me upright in my sometimes upside-down world. But, let's face it, the mai tais help a little bit too.

To Lynn Butler who had to read through a first draft of *Close Enough to Perfect*, I truly apologize. Without your comments I may never have found the right direction for my rewrite.

To early readers Candace Anderson, Jeff Cole, Cynthia Crosson, Debra Ellis, Mary-Ann DeVita Palmieri, and Robin Shtulman: thank you.

To Ellen Woodbury, who tenaciously copy-edited my memoir: thank you for taking such good care of my story.

I am grateful to my editor and publisher, Marcia Gagliardi of Haley's Publishing: you believed in my memoir from the start, which is quite astonishing to me. Your constant encouragement gave me the confidence to challenge myself. Your thoughtful and insightful comments often had me consulting a dictionary, and they were usually spot on. I thank you for taking my hand and walking me through the new and wonderful world of words.

And finally, to all those who have graciously allowed me to write about them in *Close Enough to Perfect*, I hope I did you justice.

I am blessed to have memories—both good and bad—that became my story. In a world sometimes overwhelming, our connections with one another matter most. Through such ties with family and friends, the overwhelming can become manageable.

Colophon

MVB Verdigris is a Garalde text family for the digital age. Inspired by work of sixteenth-century punchcutters Robert Granjon, Hendrik van den Keere, and Pierre Haultin, MVB Verdigris celebrates tradition but is not beholden to it. Created to deliver good typographic color as text, Mark van Bronkhorst's design meets the needs of today's designer using today's paper and press. A full-featured OpenType release with an added titling companion, it's optimized for the latest typesetting technologies too.

Garalde: the word itself sounds antique and arcane to anyone who isn't fresh out of design school, but the sort of typeface it describes is actually quite familiar to all of us. Despite its age—born fairly early in printing's history—the style has fared well. Garaldes are the typefaces of choice for books and other long reading. And so we continue to see text set in old favorites—Garamond, Sabon, and their

Venetian predecessor, Bembo. Yet many new books don't feel as handsome and readable as older books printed in the original, metal type. The problem is that digital type revivals are typically facsimiles of their metal predecessors, merely duplicating the letterforms rather than capturing the impression—both physical and emotional—that the typefaces once left on the page.

www.ingramcontent.com/pod-product-compliance
Lightning Source LLC
Chambersburg PA
CBHW061306110426
42742CB00012BA/2073